HOME BUYER'S ESSENTIALS

50 TIPS
for confident house buying

Anna Roberts MRICS

First Edition, England & Wales

Home Buyer's Essentials

DISCLAIMER

The information provided in this book, (Home Buyer's Essentials: 50 Tips for Confident House Buying), is intended for general informational purposes only and is not a substitute for specific professional advice. This book does not constitute legal, financial, or property-specific advice, and readers are strongly encouraged to seek independent professional assistance tailored to their individual circumstances.

The content of this book is relevant to property in England and Wales only and may not apply to property transactions elsewhere. Any actions taken based on the tips or suggestions contained within this book are entirely at the reader's own risk. Neither the author, A. Roberts, nor the publisher, accepts any responsibility for any loss, injury, or legal claims that may result from following the information presented.

While every effort has been made to ensure the accuracy of the information, the author and publisher make no representations or warranties regarding the completeness, accuracy, or currentness of the content. Laws, regulations, and market conditions can change, and readers should verify that any advice or practices comply with current legal requirements.

Following the tips provided in this book does not guarantee specific results or outcomes. Any links, references, or citations included were correct at the time of writing, but they may change over time.

Mentions of companies, products, or services are not endorsements unless explicitly stated, and the author may not have affiliations with the entities referenced.

This work is copyrighted to A. Roberts and may not be reproduced, distributed, or transmitted in any form or by any means, including photocopying, recording, or other electronic or mechanical methods, without prior written permission from the author.

First Edition, England & Wales
2025, GREDU
Cover image credit: canva
All rights reserved
ISBN 978-1-0369-1143-0

Home Buyer's Essentials

CONTENTS

INTRODUCTION

GENERAL

1. Why are you buying a house?
2. What is the home buying process and example delays?
3. What are the different types of surveys?
4. Who does what in the house buying process?
5. When are the various people involved?
6. How do I buy something that will be sustainable?
7. Thinking about buying a house – what to do first?
8. What is the big deal about "South Facing Gardens"?
9. What is gazumping?

HOW TO BUY

10. How do I find a house?
11. Affordable home ownership and home building schemes – what are they?
12. Should I buy a flat?
13. Should I buy a new home?
14. Should I buy "off plan"?
15. Should I buy a renovation project?
16. Should I buy a tiny home?
17. How do I buy from an auction?
18. What if the house is "unmortgageable"?
19. How do I buy a buy to let?
20. What if the house I'm buying has tenants?
21. How to buy with family/friends?

22. How to buy for a family member?
23. How do I organise the move?
24. Do I need storage?
25. Why is it good to be a "good buyer"?
26. What is a "chain"?

FINANCIALS

27. How much does the process cost?
28. Am I going to be able to afford it?
29. What are the big costs risks?
30. How do I get a mortgage?
31. What happens to my deposit?
32. How do I know if I'm buying the house for the right price?
33. What should I know about service charges?
34. What does "negative equity" mean?
35. What if I'm buying the house purely as an investment?

UNDERSTANDING THE SURVEY REPORTS

36. What are the parts of the house called?
37. Which parts will cost me the most money?
38. What is rising damp?
39. What is penetrating damp?
40. Damp or condensation and mould?
41. What is Radon?
42. What about asbestos?
43. What if there's cracks?

SEARCHES AND SERVICES

44. What if it's in an area of flood risk?

45. How do I transfer or connect Water, Drainage, Electric, Gas, Oil, Broadband, Phone?
46. What documentation could come with a house?
47. What if there's no building regulations for alterations/extensions?
48. What is a FENSA certificate?
49. What if there's no planning permission for alterations/extensions?
50. What if the loft conversion is not "official"?
51. What are Energy Performance Certificates (EPC's)?
52. What are "searches"?
53. What is a right of way?
54. What is "overage"?
55. What if there are boundary issues?
56. Who is the Land Registry?
57. What is a leasehold?
58. What is a freehold?
59. What insurance do I need?
60. What is an Architect's certificate (PCC)?
61. What if it's a listed building?
62. What if it is in an AONB or Conservation Area?
63. Why is it important to consider the surrounding land use?

GLOSSARY

REFERENCES

NOTES

INTRODUCTION

Congratulations. If you're reading this book, I'm guessing you're in some way contemplating buying a house. In 2025 that's no small achievement. You are standing where many wish they were in having some kind of plan or option to buy your own home.

There's no point sugar coating it; you're going to be in for an emotional ride. Even the most rational of home buyers find themselves frustrated when the inevitable twists and turns of buying a house play out. But fear not! This snappily titled book is here to empower you on your quest to holding those keys, and one day, relatively soon, you will gaze down at them in the palm of your hand and will breathe a sigh of relief as you embrace the next chapter of your life – you have got this.

Before we continue, I should point out this book is of most use to those people who in some way already have a plan to buy a house (and more specifically in England and Wales). This is as opposed to a book which helps people arrive at a point where financially they even have the option to buy a house. Whilst it would be a brilliant accompaniment to this book, it would require its own edition and a broader range of skillsets...and maybe even a silver bullet embedded in its pages, (truthfully it is entirely possible to buy your own home if that is what you truly desire, but you don't need me to tell you the challenges).

This book isn't exactly what it seems (you might as well start getting used to these sort of curve balls if you're going to buy a house), but this is a sweet kind of surprise......I tried, Lord knows I tried, to condense some of the most frequent things I have come across as a Chartered Surveyor, into 50 Tips, but the best I could do was 63. "So why not change the book title?" I hear you apathetically ponder.....let's face it no one was going to buy a book with the title "63 Tips for confident house buying". There's possibly some consumer psychology in there to explain it, but that's not what we are here for, so let's get on with this.

This book is written to make your life easier. Buying a home is notoriously one of the most stressful things you can do, and I would argue one of the more unnecessarily complex things in today's age, but again, that's a whole other book. The trouble is, even if you are confident in your buying journey, there could still be questions you haven't thought to ask or things you discover along the way that you're unfamiliar with.

You don't need to read the book from front to back. I would suggest familiarising yourself with the sections and skim through the titles above, then keep this book to hand throughout your buying journey ready to quickly reference, highlight, make notes on, when you come across something you're not sure on.

Finally, before we delve into the things I would like to say a huge thanks to my son, partner, parents, and all my family and friends who have supported me in writing the book and in fact have supported me throughout my whole career. It is one which has spanned over 20 years as a Building Surveyor, having grown up with parents who lived in and renovated/built houses as we lived in them, (I have also lived in my fair share of "off-site" caravans while this happened). I bought my first house, a barn conversion project when I was 22 and my love of property has never ceased. More recently I have become the founder and CEO of SelfStorageBooker.com, a site which makes it easy to find and book the self storage you need, (an incredibly helpful service when moving house (see Tip 24).

The direction of this book was shaped by current affairs, professional knowledge and experience and personal research about what home and home ownership means to people. These continue to prompt further questions about home and property, such that I may well prop my laptop up on a "Keep Calm and Carry On" tray table one evening and start planning further versions. If there's something in particular you would like to see published, or indeed if there is something you think would be worth including in the second edition of this book, please email support@explorage.com.

GENERAL

1. WHY ARE YOU BUYING A HOUSE?

"Buying a house is a significant milestone and a major financial commitment, often considered a crucial part of achieving long-term stability and financial security." – thanks Chat GPT for articulating the pressure!

I was fortunate to be brought up in a family where the concept of "house" and "home" were used quite loosely. My parents were part of the post war "survival" generation. The deposit for their first home was saved by breeding and selling piglets! Once they were married and moved into their house, they had two of their four children in close succession. Then at 25, they started their lifelong commitment to living in houses that they couldn't really afford, renovating them alongside doing their day jobs, selling them, and buying a house that was slightly better. By the time I left home I personally had lived in 9 houses, including two caravans on buildings sites; the concept of "settling" in to a "forever home" was alien to me.

Now, you may not have a paddock for raising pigs, but the point of my story is to help you to start thinking outside of the box. There is always more than one way to "skin a cat" and the same applies to buying a house. If you are saving for a deposit, then the piggy side hustle or an equivalent of it could accelerate your house buying position. The thing is to keep an open mind and start to think about what it is you really want from a house. This could help you to recognise perhaps unconsidered ways of achieving your aspirations.

A good friend of mine was bereaved by her housing situation. Living in London, single, mid 30's, on a distinctly average salary you will not be surprised to find she spent most of her income on a room in a house share. There was one snag however. It was a house share between her and a single friend; and every time the friend found a serious relationship, my friend would be left worrying about how and whether she could keep a roof over her head, when her friend inevitably moved out to live with the beloved. It was exhausting. Incidentally, my friend befriended (bear with me…) a guy who lived on a houseboat – a lifestyle which it turned out she loved. She had also heard my tales about living in caravans growing up… Her mindset about what a house meant to her started to change and in the space of several months, she managed to secure a £40,000 loan from her brother, scraped together the money for a boat survey and annual mooring fees, and she became the proud owner of a houseboat on the Thames. 5 years on and she still adores her floating home. She feels secure and empowered and can now focus on other aspects of her life.

Granted, buying a houseboat or living in a renovation project might not be your cup of tea. The point here, however, is to really prompt you to think about why you truly want a house, or indeed want to move to a different one, and what features of the new property will be particularly important to you.

A house could be one of the biggest financial investments you ever make. Whilst my mother has a point when she says, "it's just a house, you can always sell it" (see "Financials" first), depending on your driving reason for buying a house, it can dramatically affect the type of property that is best for you to invest in right now.

On that note, one more little story before we get into the detail.

A friend had reached the fortunate position of being able to buy their first home with their partner. They had sacrificed a fair bit to save up a deposit and were excited to finally be able to get onto what felt like an increasingly high first rung of the property ladder. In their excitement, they looked at a range of houses that met their criteria. It had to be close to pretty dog walks and commutable to work. Eventually they settled on a nicely renovated stone cottage that in truth could do them for life. They asked me to take a look at it; it was a lovely house that had been well maintained and extended. There were inevitably a few "quirks" however, which meant that keeping on top of various maintenance tasks was going to be especially important. I suggested they consider not just the house but the lifestyle they wanted over the next 5-10 years and how they saw the house fitting into that. After some thought and further house hunting, they eventually changed their mind and settled on a very low maintenance first home. This one was a typical 1980's masonry box. But it was in the location they wanted, and it had the potential to receive a relatively straight forward cosmetic renovation to add a bit of value to it. They said that in coming to their decision they had decided they would still like to do some travelling. They wanted a house that was low maintenance and easy to repair should they decide to rent it out. They also wanted something more modest that would allow them to still save and in the longer term enable them to buy a more substantial family home when they were ready.

Point to note from the story above; they took the age-old route of building value in a property, i.e. they bought a run-down house (in this case just a bit dated), in a great location, and renovated it. It is true what they say about location being the most important thing to consider. You could add a high-spec extension to a house in an undesirable location, but it would still only fetch a limited price. As with every sale, know the market you'll eventually be selling to and consider what type of house they would want to buy.....even if it is your home in the meantime.

Hopefully your mind is now somewhat more open to the reasons you are buying a house…. and hey, I'm with you, there is a lot to be said for owning your own home that you love. Here are some of the main reasons people tend to buy:

Investment and financial stability

One of the main reasons people buy a house is the potential for long-term financial stability and investment growth. Unlike renting, where monthly payments are made without return on investment, mortgage payments contribute towards owning a tangible asset. Over time, as you pay down your mortgage, you also build equity in your property. Additionally, property values tend to appreciate over the long term, which can provide a significant return on investment when you decide to sell. Historically, property has been a reliable way to build wealth, and many see home ownership as a key part of their financial planning. Having said that, there are plenty of financial advisors who would say there are also benefits to not owning and recommend instead investing that same money in other, potentially more lucrative or stable opportunities. So, if you are purely buying a house from an investment perspective, take some advice from a professional authorised by the Financial Conduct Authority (FCA), and consider ALL options before committing.

Control and personalisation

Homeownership offers a level of control and personalisation that arguably renting cannot. As a homeowner, you have the freedom and incentive to renovate, decorate, and make improvements to your property as you see fit. This ability to customise your living space allows you to create a home that truly reflects your tastes, preferences, and needs. Whether it's landscaping the garden, installing a new kitchen, or adding an extension, owning a home provides the opportunity to create a space that feels uniquely yours.

Stability and security

For many owning a home provides a sense of stability and security. Unlike renting, where leases can be terminated and rent prices can increase, (although recent rental legislation is set to improve this situation for tenants somewhat), owning a home offers more predictable monthly payments (if you have a fixed-rate mortgage), and the security of knowing that the property is yours. This stability is particularly important for families, as it allows for long-term planning and the establishment of roots in a community.

Pride of ownership and a sense of place

Whilst being one of the less tangible factors, there is a certain satisfaction that comes with owning your own home. It's a significant achievement and often represents years of hard work and saving. This sense of accomplishment and pride can contribute to overall happiness and satisfaction with life. There is also the relative safety of having your own personal constant space in this busy world. From my own research on general homeowner sentiment, 62% of 122 people said they saw their home as their "sanctuary/kingdom". Homeownership is also seen in many cultures as a sign of success and stability, which can be personally fulfilling.

Building equity

As you pay off your mortgage, you build equity in your home. Equity is the difference between the market value of your home and the amount you owe on your mortgage. This equity can be a valuable financial resource, offering opportunities to borrow against it for significant expenses, such as home improvements, other investments, or emergency funds – but this is subject to your affordability. Equity can also provide a financial cushion in retirement but is no replacement for a pension and it is recommended that if you haven't already, you take financial advice in this respect.

Legacy and inheritance

A home can serve as a legacy to pass down to future generations. It can provide financial security for your children or other heirs and can be an important part of estate planning. Passing on a home can give your family a significant financial advantage, helping them with their own housing needs or providing a substantial asset. But again, there are pitfalls that you will need experienced financial advice on if this is your main driver. Inheritance tax can be a huge blow if you and your family haven't planned and prepared for it.

2. WHAT IS THE HOME BUYING PROCESS AND EXAMPLE DELAYS?

Buying a house tends to follow several steps, and the smoother each one goes, the smoother the overall transaction. The industry still reports that between a quarter and a third of all property transaction fall through because of either the buyer or seller pulling out. Therefore, it is sensible to pro-actively and positively work through the process as efficiently as possible until you have completion, or at least until you have exchanged contracts.

I cannot over emphasise how useful it is to keep a diary/log with the dates and details of all communications and all outcomes of them, (in particular any promises or agreements), so that you can easily reference back to them when you need to chase people up – which you will....a lot.

At each point of contact it is helpful for you both to agree the date by which the next action or communication will take place, so that you can take charge of keeping the process moving forward and quickly identify any possible issues on the horizon. The sooner you are aware of these the less disruptive it is likely to be to you both emotionally and financially.

It is worth noting that the process below is representative of you buying a house without selling your current house to pay for it. If you are in a chain (see Tip 26), naturally there are more complications and risks, but the basic principles are the same.

THE HOUSE BUYING PROCESS

1. Determine your budget

The first step is understanding how much you can afford. This involves evaluating your savings for a deposit, income, current expenses, and any debts. Online mortgage calculators can help you estimate the amount you might be able to borrow and the monthly repayments. You may also already have a house to sell; if so, ask a few estate agents around to give you an indication of the market value so you can factor that into your budget. Don't forget to plan in costs associated to the house buying and moving process itself (see Tip 27). Keep a list of all the different fees you will have to pay. You will be surprised how much they add up.

2. Get a mortgage agreement in principle

Before you start viewing properties, if you need a mortgage, it's wise to obtain a mortgage agreement in principle from a lender (see Tip 30). This is a statement from a mortgage provider indicating how much they might lend you, based on your financial situation. While not a guarantee, it helps show sellers you are serious and financially prepared.

3. Search for properties

With your budget and mortgage in principle, you can begin searching for properties. Use online property portals, visit local estate agents, and explore neighbourhoods that interest you. It's important to view multiple properties to understand what is available in your price range.

4. Viewings

Schedule viewings for properties that meet your criteria. During these visits, take note of the property's condition, layout, and any potential issues. It's also a good opportunity to get a feel for the neighbourhood and nearby amenities.

5. Make an offer

Once you find a suitable property, you can make an offer through the estate agent or directly to the vendor depending on how they are selling it. The offer should be in writing/via email and should state a date by when you expect to hear back, (don't chase before this date or you could seem too keen).

It is sensible to make the offer subject to conditions such as the sale of your current home, subject to a satisfactory survey, or subject to exchanging by a certain date. Negotiation may be necessary to agree on a final price and terms. It helps if you can demonstrate you are a "good buyer" (see Tip 25), and gather "evidence" to substantiate your offer, such as the sales prices from similar properties in similar areas.

Be aware that as in most negotiations, in this case the estate agent/seller could use various methods to help secure the best deal for them. Examples could include implying a sense of urgency, uniqueness or unrealistic buyer expectations. This isn't personal and indeed their statements may be accurate. It is simply important to keep a clear head and focus on the outcome that you want.

6. Offer accepted and solicitor instructed

If your offer is accepted, you need to formally apply for your mortgage. Your lender will conduct a valuation of the property to ensure it is worth the loan amount. This is also the stage where you will instruct a solicitor or conveyancer to handle the legal aspects of the purchase.

7. Surveys and checks

Depending on the property and your lender's requirements, you may need to commission a property survey. There are different levels of surveys, from basic valuations to detailed building surveys that highlight potential structural issues (see Tip 3).

Your solicitor will conduct "searches" (see Tip 52), to check for any potential legal or local issues. At this stage they may also unearth concerns like unfavourable clauses in the title documents (see "Searches and Services"), or high flood or subsidence risks for example, which could mean you choose not to continue with the purchase.

The solicitor will identify any issues and will create a list of enquiries that require further investigation/clarification.

8. Solicitor's report

Once all searches and enquiries are complete, your solicitor will prepare a report for you usually called a "Report on Title". Along with the seller's property information form (see Tip 46), this report provides you with all the information the solicitor has formed about the property to allow you to make an informed decision about whether to buy it. The report doesn't offer an opinion.

If you are satisfied with the results, you can proceed to sign contracts and send your solicitor the deposit monies – typically 10% of the purchase price. You will need to sign/return:

- Contract of Sale
- TR1 Form (see Tip 46)
- Stamp Duty Land Tax declaration form/Land Transaction tax form (see Tip 27)
- Mortgage deed (if applicable)
- Deed of covenant or other deeds (if applicable)
- Building insurance (if requested by solicitor/lender)

Once the solicitors have received and confirmed all the necessary documents (see Tip 46), have been signed and returned, they will negotiate a day when the parties will "exchange contracts".

9. Exchange of contracts

Arguably one of the most exciting points in the process. Once you and the seller have exchanged contracts, you are legally committed to the sale/purchase.

Your solicitor will have some pre-exchange checks to make including;

- Obtaining your consent to exchange, usually via email. This typically happens every day e.g. if for some reason you don't exchange today and you have just given consent, if the exchange is pushed back until tomorrow you will be asked for it again in the morning.
- Bankruptcy checks on you.
- Confirm that mortgage funds can be released in time for completion.
- Notification to Land Registry.

- Confirm certain points with seller's solicitor e.g. confirming vacant possession.

Once they are satisfied, they will inform the seller's solicitor that they are ready to exchange. The two solicitors will then confirm all essential details e.g. purchase price, parties' details and the completion date, (this can either be a set date, or on notice).

Once all this is confirmed, they will note the date and time on the contracts and the exchange of contracts is now complete.

10. Completion

Typically, around a week after exchange, (but could be anywhere from the same day to 6 months after), and usually before 11am on the agreed completion date, the remaining funds to purchase the property are transferred by your solicitor to the seller, and you will be informed.

If you are taking out a mortgage, the mortgage money is received by your solicitor before being paid out – these, and any other necessary monies, could be sent to your solicitor the day before to reduce the risk of delay to completion.

Once the seller has then left the property and provided vacant possession their solicitor will authorise whoever is holding the keys to release them to you.

You can now go and collect the keys to your new home and move in.

11. Post-completion

After completion, your solicitor will handle the final legalities, such as paying the Stamp Duty Land Tax.

For you it is time to move in and start setting up utilities and services in your name. As well as remembering to pause, reflect and celebrate what you have achieved.

EXAMPLE DELAYS

- Issues in the "chain" (see Tip 26).

- Mortgage lender delays e.g. if their valuation is lower than the agreed purchase price you may need to renegotiate, find additional funds or walk away from the purchase.

- Searches taking longer than expected to return (see Tip 52).

- If there are unexpected survey or search results that require further investigation or renegotiation.

- If the house is in legal processes following the death of the owner and the Grant of Probate or Letters of Administration have not yet been issued allowing the property to be sold; 6-12+ months delay.

- If the property is not already registered with the Land Registry; 4-16+ months delay (see Tip 56).

- If there are disputes over the boundary position.

- Unresolved or contested points in the property deeds/title register/title plan.

- Discovery of the lack of relevant statutory consents e.g. for previous alterations (see Tip 49).

- For leasehold properties, delays in obtaining any necessary freeholder consents (see Tip 57).

- If the property is registered under one of the affordable housing schemes (see Tip 11), such as "Help to Buy" (ended in England in 2023), there will be extra processes and checks.

- Proof of funds checking process (anti-money laundering legislation), especially when a mortgage is not required for the purchase, or money used for the purchase is coming from overseas.

Try to highlight any potential delays early in the buying process by asking estate agents, solicitors and lenders questions which may flag up issues in advance, e.g. ask about the example delay scenarios above. This could help to avoid them being discovered at the last minute when the stakes are higher, and time is more sensitive.

3. WHAT ARE THE DIFFERENT TYPES OF SURVEYS?

There are many different types of surveys a person buying a house could have carried out and the surveyors themselves, and your solicitor, should be able to advise on the most suitable.

A valuation survey is standard practice, and this is usually required by a mortgage lender. Many people confuse this survey with other types because it is the most common with homebuyers.

Other surveys are helpful particularly in respect of the building itself. Whilst they may not relate to the value of the building as it is currently; they can save you a lot of money in the long run. For example, if an RICS Level 2 survey reports that some significant unobvious repair work is required, you may feel you need to renegotiate on the offer price in light of this new information (be prepared to offer estimates for the work to substantiate your new offer). The survey could also help you to plan for longer term maintenance budgets so that you can decide whether you still want the house and can afford it.

Mortgage valuation survey

A mortgage lender is likely to instruct a valuation survey. This could be either done from desktop research without visiting the property or could be done with a valuation surveyor visiting the property itself. The lender will determine the type they require based on their own criteria. Usually, you will be charged a fee for the valuation survey.

RICS Level 1 Condition Survey

The Condition Report is the most basic type of survey and is suitable for modern homes in good condition. It provides an overview of the property's condition, highlighting any urgent defects that need attention but does not go into detail about repairs or maintenance. This survey uses a simple 'traffic light' system to indicate the condition of different parts of the property: green (no repair needed), amber (defects that need repairing or replacing but are not considered serious or urgent), and red (serious defects needing urgent repair).

RICS Level 2 Home Survey (RICS Level 2 Home Buyer Survey)

The RICS Level 2 Home Survey is more detailed than the Condition Report and is suitable for conventional properties in reasonable condition. It includes all the elements of a Condition Report but also offers advice on necessary repairs and ongoing maintenance. It can potentially include a market valuation and insurance rebuild cost; however, these need to be requested as an extra and it will depend on the type of surveyor, (there are many Chartered Surveyor types), as to whether they will undertake this work. The Home Survey report does not include in-depth structural analysis, so it's not suitable for older or more complex properties. Often home buyers choose to instruct their own

Level 2 survey by an independent Chartered Surveyor, (i.e. separate to the mortgage valuation).

RICS Level 3 Building Survey

The RICS Level 3 Building Survey is the most comprehensive of the standard RICS survey types and is ideal for older, larger, or unusually constructed properties, as well as those in especially poor condition. It provides a detailed analysis of the property's structure and condition, including visible and potential defects. The surveyor will thoroughly inspect all accessible areas, offering detailed advice on repairs, maintenance, and potential future issues.

New-build snagging survey

For new-build properties, a snagging survey identifies defects, incomplete work, or issues that need to be addressed by the housing developer. This survey ensures that the property meets the expected standards and that any necessary corrections are made before you move in.

Specific defects report

If you have concerns about a particular issue with a property which you would like to have investigated in isolation such as wiring, asbestos or structural movement, you can commission a specific survey in that respect. This survey focuses on the particular problem/building element and will provide detailed information and recommendations for addressing it. This type of survey will require a specialist surveyor or engineer in the respective field. They will often have different names or terminology for the type of survey/report, but don't worry too much about this, as long as you are confident the scope of their instruction covers everything it might need.

4. WHO DOES WHAT IN THE HOUSE BUYING PROCESS?

The house-buying process involves multiple parties, each with distinct roles and responsibilities, below is a summary of some of the key players and their main roles:

Buyer
- Determines budget and financial readiness.
- Secures a mortgage agreement in principle.
- Searches for properties and attends viewings.
- Makes offers and negotiates with sellers, (often via an estate agent).
- Instructs a solicitor or conveyancer.
- Arranges property surveys.
- Finalises the mortgage application.
- Signs contracts and completes the purchase.
- Plans utilities and admin/address switches and organises and sometimes does the packing and moving themselves.

Seller
- Prepares the property for sale.
- Markets the property e.g. through an estate agent.
- Provides access to the property for viewings, surveys etc. or gives agent access for this.
- Negotiates offers with potential buyers, (often via an estate agent).
- Provides necessary property information and documentation.
- Works with a solicitor or conveyancer to handle the legal aspects of the sale.

- Makes arrangements for utilities and admin/address switches and organises, or sometimes does the packing and moving themselves.

Estate Agent
- Suggests a value to market the property.
- Markets the property on behalf of the seller.
- Arranges and conducts viewings.
- Facilitates communication between the buyer and seller.
- Assists in negotiating offers and sale terms.

Solicitor/Conveyancer
- Deals with the legal aspects of buying or selling a property.
- A solicitor can handle all aspects of property law, including disputes, while a conveyancer specialises only in property transactions.
- Solicitors are regulated by the SRA, and conveyancers by the CLC.
- Conducts property searches and legal checks. Prepares and investigates a list of enquiries about the property/ seller/terms of sale.
- Prepares and reviews contracts.
- Prepares relevant legal documents and those which require signing (see Tip 46).
- Manages the exchange of contracts and transfer of funds.
- Registers/updates the property's Title with the Land Registry.
- Arranges and settles Stamp Duty Land Tax/Land Transaction Tax costs from the funds.
- Recommends other professional advice where necessary.

Mortgage Lender
- Assesses the buyer's financial situation and offers a mortgage agreement in principle.
- Conducts a property valuation to ensure it is worth the loan amount.
- Finalises the mortgage offer and provides the necessary funds for the purchase.
- Sets the terms and conditions of the mortgage.

Surveyor
- Conducts property surveys relative to the scope of the survey type (see Tip 3).
- Provides detailed reports and recommendations.
- Provides specialist advice in respect of the property.

Mortgage Broker
- Assists the buyer in finding and securing the best mortgage deal.
- Provides advice on different mortgage products and lenders.
- Manages the mortgage application process on behalf of the buyer.

5. WHEN ARE THE VARIOUS PEOPLE INVOLVED?

Timing is important in the house-buying process. The sooner you can start to "warm up" the people you are likely to need and when, the more chance you have of them flagging up early considerations which could save you time, money and headache in the longer term.

Be mindful if you are in direct communication with the seller to share and confirm any agreements/understandings with your solicitor. They will advise whether these have any impact on the buying process or if there is anything which may need to be confirmed in writing.

It is also worth noting that professional rules of conduct prohibit the seller's solicitor from communicating directly with you, or your solicitor communicating directly with the seller. It is therefore better to direct all communication via your own solicitor/conveyancer. This makes it even more important that you use a professional you have confidence in.

Before property search

- Mortgage lender or broker: Secure a mortgage agreement in principle to understand your budget and demonstrate financial readiness to sellers.

- Financial advisor: If needed, consult a financial advisor to assess your financial situation and plan your budget.

- Estate agent: If you have your own property to sell/rent, gaining initial advise from an estate agent who may market it for you will help you to determine your budget and potentially gain more of an understanding of how quickly you will be able to move. This will also help you to think about whether you want to make alternative moving arrangements rather than being in a "chain" e.g. sell your current home and rent somewhere in meantime to be able to move faster on buying the new home (See Tip 26).

During property search

- Estate agent: Engage with estate agents to help find suitable properties and arrange viewings. Get added to waiting lists especially if you are in a high demand area.

- Property developer: If buying a new home, meeting with the property developer may give you an opportunity to think about any variations you may like to request to the final house specification, e.g. tiling colours.

After finding a property

- **Solicitor/conveyancer:** Instruct a solicitor or conveyancer once your offer is accepted. They will handle the legal aspects of the purchase including conducting necessary searches, reviewing contracts, and addressing any legal concerns.

- **Mortgage lender:** Finalise your mortgage application and secure a mortgage offer (see Tip 30). The lender will conduct a property valuation during this stage.

- **Surveyor:** Arrange a property survey (see Tip 3), to assess the condition of the property and identify potential issues.

- **Estate Agent:** It is helpful to keep the seller's estate agent up to speed on progress, particularly if there are any blockages which seem to be coming from the seller's side. This will also demonstrate that you are equally keen on reaching exchange of contracts.

Before completion

- **Solicitor/conveyancer:** Manage the exchange of contracts and coordinate the transfer of funds. They will also register the property with the Land Registry after completion.

- **Insurance provider:** Arrange for home insurance to start from the completion date, as this is often a mortgage condition.

Post-completion

- **Solicitor/conveyancer:** Finalise any remaining legalities, such as paying Stamp Duty Land Tax and ensuring all documentation is properly filed.

6. HOW DO I BUY SOMETHING THAT WILL BE SUSTAINABLE?

Knowing your new home will be sustainable both from an environmental and from a "running costs" perspective is paramount in many buyer's minds.

Sustainable home buying involves considering the environmental impact, energy efficiency, and long-term living costs. Here are some steps to help you in your search:

Energy efficiency

- Look for homes with high Energy Performance Certificate (EPC) ratings. An A or B rating indicates excellent energy efficiency. The EPC will also give details of each of the building components and how they fair from an energy performance perspective.

- Check for energy-efficient features such as double or triple glazing, proper insulation, more modern energy-efficient heating systems, and LED lighting.

Sustainable materials

- Consider properties built with sustainable materials like reclaimed wood, recycled metal, and low-VOC (volatile organic compounds) paints and finishes. These materials reduce environmental impact and improve indoor air quality.

Renewable energy sources

- Homes with solar panels (photovoltaics aka. PV), solar thermal panels (thermal voltaic), wind turbines and air or ground-source heat pumps for example, are usually more sustainable and can significantly reduce energy bills.

- See if the property has an efficient, renewable energy heating system such as biomass boilers or solar water heating.

Water efficiency

- Look for properties with water-saving features like low-flow taps, dual-flush toilets, and rainwater harvesting systems.
- Consider homes with greywater recycling systems that reuse water from sinks, showers, and washing machines for irrigation or flushing toilets.

Location and transport

- Choose a location with good public transport links, cycling paths, and walkable amenities. This reduces reliance on cars and lowers your carbon footprint.
- Proximity to services like schools, shops, and healthcare can also reduce travel needs and enhance community sustainability.

Green spaces

- Properties with gardens or nearby green spaces support biodiversity and provide opportunities for growing your own food, reducing your environmental impact.
- Consider homes with "green roofs" i.e. roofs that have vegetation planted on them or living walls that help insulate the property and support urban biodiversity.

Building orientation

- South-facing properties maximise natural light, reducing the need for artificial lighting and heating. Orientation can significantly impact energy efficiency.

- Homes designed to harness natural ventilation can reduce the need for mechanical ventilation or air conditioning and improve indoor air quality.

Community initiatives

- Some developments have community energy projects, shared green spaces, and collective waste management systems. Participating in these initiatives can enhance sustainability.

- Research community engagement in sustainability practices, such as recycling programs and local food production.

Smart home technology

- Smart thermostats, energy monitoring systems, and automated lighting can optimise energy use and improve the overall efficiency of your home.

- Consider properties with integrated home automation systems that manage energy consumption and enhance convenience.

Futureproofing

- Think about future sustainability improvements you can make, such as adding solar panels, upgrading insulation, or installing a heat pump.

- Properties with potential for extension or modification can adapt to future needs and sustainability enhancements.

Financial incentives

- Investigate government grants, subsidies, and incentives for energy-efficient home improvements or renewable energy installations.

- Some mortgage providers offer green mortgages with better rates for energy-efficient homes or financing for sustainable upgrades.

Sustainable practices

- Adopt sustainable living practices such as composting, recycling, and reducing water and energy use.

- Engage with local sustainability initiatives and support businesses that prioritise environmental responsibility.

7. THINKING ABOUT BUYING A HOUSE – WHAT TO DO FIRST?

First things first, read Tip 1; once you have done that, we may continue.

1. Assess your financial situation

- Evaluate your savings, income, expenses, and existing debts to determine how much you can afford for a deposit and monthly mortgage payments.

- Aim to save at least 10-20% of the property price for a deposit to secure better mortgage rates. Usually, the more deposit you can put down the better.

2. Check your credit score

- Your credit score significantly impacts your ability to get a mortgage, and the interest rates offered. Obtain a copy of your credit report and ensure there are no errors. If there are errors prepare evidence to support your case and inform the credit bureau in writing/email. They should have a process for dealing with disputes.

- Improve your credit score by paying off unfavourable debts, reducing credit card balances, and avoiding new credit applications in the months leading up to your mortgage application. If you've never had a credit card this could also affect your score because there's little credit history on you.... I don't make the rules! There are plenty of resources online with tips on how to improve your score.

3. Research mortgage options

- Explore different mortgage types and lenders. Fixed-rate mortgages provide stability over an agreed period of time, such as 2-10 years, with consistent payments, while variable-rate mortgages may offer lower initial rates but can fluctuate.

- Consider consulting a mortgage broker for personalised advice and to help find the best deal for your circumstances.

4. Get a mortgage agreement in principle

- Obtain a mortgage agreement in principle (AIP) from a lender. This shows sellers you are serious and financially prepared, making you a more attractive buyer.

- An AIP is not a formal mortgage offer but gives a good indication of how much you can borrow.

5. Define your requirements

- Make a list of your must-haves and nice-to-haves in a property, such as location, number of bedrooms, garden size, and proximity to schools or transport links.

- Consider your long-term needs and how the property can accommodate potential changes, such as a growing family or working from home (again, if you haven't already read Tip 1).

6. Research the market

- Study the local property market to understand price trends, availability, and the types of properties within your budget.

- Use online property portals, estate agents, local contacts, local social media groups and local newspapers to gather information.

7. Choose a solicitor or conveyancer

- Find a reputable solicitor or conveyancer to handle the legal aspects of your purchase. They will manage contracts, property searches, and liaise with the seller's solicitor.

- Getting recommendations from friends or family and checking reviews can help you choose a reliable solicitor, but it's also worth having a chat with who would be representing you to get a sense of whether you can work with them.

- Usually, you would instruct your solicitor once you have had an offer on a house accepted.

8. Start viewing properties

- Begin viewing properties that meet your criteria. Keep an open mind and view a variety of homes to get a feel for what is available in your price range.

- It's worth looking at a couple of properties that are slightly outside of your criteria too. You may find your dream home and actually be prepared to compromise on one of your "essential" requirements or work around it.

- If you are in a fast-paced high demand market, you will need to be on the ball to make sure you know immediately, or even before, of any suitable properties coming to the open market. It helps if you position yourself as a "good buyer" (see Tip 25). It may also help to build good relationships with estate agents, ensure you are on their mailing lists and make sure you have push notifications activated on your phone for any new property alerts you might have set up on apps such as Right Move or Zoopla. You could even try placing a classified ad for your perfect property but be wary of rogue responders.

- Take notes and photos during viewings to help remember key details and compare properties. If you are taking photos, it is courteous to ask the seller's/agent's permission before hand.

- Find out what you can about the property condition and any work that may need to be done in the near future. For example, if the boiler is old and inefficient, this could end up being a big expense in the early days of living in your new home.

9. Make an offer

- When you find a suitable property, make an offer through the estate agent. Be prepared to negotiate on price and terms based on your budget and the property's condition (see Tip 2).

- Having a mortgage agreement in principle can strengthen your position in negotiations (see Tip 25 for what makes a good buyer).

10. Arrange a survey

- Once your offer is accepted, arrange for a property survey to identify any potential issues. Choose a survey type based on the property's age, condition, and your concerns (see Tip 3).

- The survey results can inform further negotiations or decisions about the purchase.

11. Finalise mortgage application

- This would often coincide with point 10 above.

- Submit a formal mortgage application to your chosen lender, providing all required documentation. The lender will conduct a valuation of the property as part of this process.

- Ensure all paperwork is complete and accurate to avoid delays.

12. Stay organised

- Keep track of all paperwork, deadlines, and communications with your solicitor, estate agent, and mortgage lender.

- Regularly follow up to ensure everything is progressing smoothly and address any issues promptly.

- This is your house purchase, and you need to drive it. Fortune favours the efficient and swift.

8. WHAT IS THE BIG DEAL ABOUT "SOUTH FACING GARDENS"?

Here in the UK, where even the first glimpse of sunlight has us baring all and firing up the BBQ, south-facing gardens are highly sought after. In fairness there are compelling reasons; related to sunlight exposure, gardening potential, and overall enjoyment of outdoor space:

Sunlight exposure

- South-facing gardens receive the most sunlight throughout the day, especially during the peak hours of mid-morning to late afternoon. This consistent exposure to sunlight makes the garden warmer and more inviting for outdoor activities.

- In the northern hemisphere i.e. here in the UK, the sun rises in the east, moves through the southern part of the sky, and sets in the west. Therefore, a garden facing south will benefit from direct sunlight for the longest period.

Gardening potential

- For gardening enthusiasts, a south-facing garden offers optimal conditions for growing a wide variety of plants, flowers, and vegetables. Many plants thrive with ample sunlight, leading to better growth, vibrant blooms, and higher yields of fruits and vegetables.

- South-facing gardens provide the perfect environment for sun-loving plants, such as tomatoes, peppers, and various flowers that require full sun to flourish.

Energy efficiency

- Homes with south-facing gardens can also benefit from better natural light inside the house. Large windows facing the garden can capture sunlight, reducing the need for artificial lighting and potentially lowering energy bills.

- During winter, south-facing windows can help warm the interior of the home, contributing to energy efficiency and comfort.

Outdoor living

- South-facing gardens are ideal for outdoor living spaces, such as patios, decks, and seating areas. The extended hours of sunlight make these spaces more usable and enjoyable for relaxing, entertaining, and dining.

- These gardens can also provide a more pleasant environment for children to play and for hosting social gatherings with family and friends.

Property value

- The desirability of south-facing gardens can positively impact property value. Many buyers specifically look for properties with this feature, willing to pay a premium for the associated benefits.

- Estate agents often highlight south-facing gardens in property listings, knowing that this feature can attract more interest and potentially lead to quicker sales.

Seasonal enjoyment

- A south-facing garden allows homeowners to make the most of the UK's relatively short summer season. With longer days of sunlight, residents can enjoy more time outdoors, soaking up the sun and engaging in various activities.

- Even during the cooler months, a south-facing garden can provide a warmer microclimate, making it more usable throughout the year.

Psychological benefits

- Sunlight exposure is reported to have positive effects on mood and mental health. Spending time in a sunny south-facing garden could help reduce stress, boost mood, and improve overall well-being.

- The natural light and warmth create a welcoming and uplifting environment, arguably contributing to a better quality of life – if you like that sort of thing!

Reduced dampness

- The more consistent sunlight helps keep the garden drier and less prone to dampness and mould, which can be common issues in shaded areas. This can lead to a more pleasant outdoor environment and less maintenance.

9. WHAT IS GAZUMPING?

As a child I would often hear the word "gazumped" as my parents heatedly discussed their latest property shenanigans, but I thought it was some form of medical ailment.

Gazumping is a term used in the UK property market to describe a situation where a seller accepts an offer from a buyer, but then subsequently accepts another, usually higher, offer from a new buyer, thus gazumping the first buyer. This practice can cause significant frustration and financial loss for the original buyer, who may have already invested time and money into the purchase process.

How gazumping happens

- After an offer is accepted and the sale is progressing, another buyer may approach the seller with a higher offer or a quicker completion for example. The seller may decide to accept this new offer, leaving the original buyer without the property.

- This typically occurs before the exchange of contracts, as the sale is not legally binding until contracts are exchanged in the UK.

Impact on buyers

- Financial loss; the original buyer may have incurred costs for surveys, legal fees, and mortgage arrangement fees, which are non-refundable.

- Gazumping is emotionally distressing, particularly if the buyer has invested a lot of effort and has become attached to the property. (Note. Please don't start buying furniture for your new home until you have completed).

- The buyer needs to start the property search process again, which can be time-consuming and frustrating.

Reasons for gazumping

- Market conditions; in a hot property market with high demand and limited supply, sellers are more likely to receive multiple offers, increasing the risk of gazumping.

- Sellers looking to achieve the highest possible price for their property may be more inclined to entertain higher offers, even after accepting an initial offer.

- Seller has some new situation arise which means they may wish to move to another, possibly quicker, buyer.

- In the UK, until contracts are exchanged, neither party is legally bound to the sale, allowing sellers to change their minds.

Preventing gazumping

- Being in procession of a "mortgage agreement in principle" shows you are a serious buyer and can proceed quickly, making you more attractive to sellers.

- Establishing a good rapport and relationship with the seller and demonstrating your commitment to the purchase can reduce the likelihood of gazumping. Potentially even sharing a little of your personal reasons for wanting the property could go some way in gaining their loyalty to you.

Home Buyer's Essentials

- Some buyers and sellers enter into a lock-out, (or exclusivity) agreement, where both parties agree not to negotiate with other buyers for a certain period. However, these agreements are not very common and can be difficult to enforce.

- Moving quickly through the purchase process can reduce the window of opportunity for gazumping. Ensure all necessary documents and funds are ready to expedite the exchange of contracts. Once again fortune favours the efficient and swift.

- Some buyers opt for home-buying insurance that covers costs incurred if the sale falls through due to gazumping.

HOW TO BUY

10. HOW DO I FIND A HOUSE?

Start by keeping an open mind as to how you might find it. Also put yourself firmly in the driving seat and don't be put off by a property just because it's been on the market for a while, and you assume there is something wrong with it. It is these sorts of scenarios that can sometimes lead to you getting the best deal and building the most value in your home.

Trawling Right Move and other such sites will certainly give you a broad view of what's available, but if you're in a high demand area or looking for something a bit more particular it's time to let your most magnificent manifesting powers loose and start thinking outside the box.

Online property portals

- e.g. Rightmove, Zoopla, OnTheMarket, PrimeLocation etc.
- Create alerts for new listings that match your criteria.
- Use advanced search filters to narrow down properties by price, size, type, and location.
- If available, take advantage of virtual tours to view properties remotely and quickly.
- It's easy to get lost in these search results so try and think more tactically. For example, sort by date listed – oldest, this will show you which properties have been on the market the longest and therefore which sellers may, (I emphasise *may*), be more open to negotiation.

- Don't rely solely on the new property alerts. Whilst they are useful, a simple tweak of a property listing could mean it suddenly falls within your search criteria.

Estate agents

- Visit or call local estate agents' offices to discuss your requirements.

- Get on their mailing list for early notification of new properties.

- Estate agents could be the first gatekeeper in determining what the seller considers a "good buyer" (see Tip 25). Yes, they will want the commission, but it doesn't hurt to put your best foot forward and sell yourself! Subconsciously most people like dealing with people they like, and they will probably work harder for you if you can be good to deal with, open minded, efficient and paint yourself as the buyer that will make their job easier and more profitable for them.

Auction houses

- Property auctions can be a great way to find a building which you can add value to. They have some specific legal requirements however and can be risky if you are not fully informed and prepared, so get some expert advice beforehand.

- For many people auctions are not an option, since it can be risky and complicated to raise the finances swiftly; many auction goers are therefore cash buyers.

- It's important to make sure you don't get carried away and bid more than you can afford. Auction house fees can also be a nasty sting if you haven't fully factored them in.

- You can research property auctions for potential houses on various websites and indeed many property auctions are now online rather than in a physical room.

- Download auction catalogues, legal packs and attend viewings before the auction date.

- Be prepared to act quickly and have finances in order, as auction purchases require prompt payment.

Local newspapers and magazines

- Check the property sections of local newspapers and lifestyle magazines for listings.

- Look for classified ads.

Social media and online communities

- Browse listings on Facebook Marketplace for properties for sale. I found a great "off-market" (i.e. not with an estate agent), house this way. It was identified as the wrong, (worse) location than it was, and the main image was the back door surrounded by pebble dash not the bay windowed front. Needless to say, we moved quickly on the purchase.

- Online classified ads type sites; Preloved, Gumtree, Vivastreet, Freeads, Friday-ad.

- Join local community groups and forums on platforms like Facebook, Reddit, and Nextdoor for leads. Also keep an eye out for Landlord Groups, where private landlords might share they are disposing of their housing portfolio.

- Network with real estate professionals who might have insider knowledge of upcoming listings. LinkedIn could be handy for this, but increasingly estate agents are becoming more visible on Instagram and TikTok too.

Direct contact

- Distribute leaflets in desired areas indicating your interest in buying a property.

- Knock on doors in neighbourhoods you like to inquire if owners are considering selling – obviously be careful with this one and put your personal safety first. Some people may not take kindly to having a stranger arrive unannounced asking to buy their house!

- Inform friends, family, and colleagues about your search. Personal networks can sometimes reveal off-market opportunities. Hairdressers, corner shop owners, postal workers will often have a close ear to the ground, whether they like it or not!

Developers and new build sales offices

- New developments: contact developers directly to inquire about new builds. Developers like Barratt Homes, Taylor Wimpey, and Persimmon Homes have dedicated sales teams.

- Show homes: visit show homes to get a feel for the quality and layout of new builds.

Government and local authority

- Look for information on affordable housing and shared ownership schemes on government websites or by ringing or calling in their offices.

- Some local councils have lists of properties for sale or rent, including affordable housing options.

Property search agencies

- Hire a property search agent who specialises in finding homes for buyers. They can sometimes provide access to off-market properties and negotiate on your behalf.

Relocation services

- If you are planning to use relocation services if you're moving from another area or country, they sometimes offer other support, including finding a home, schooling, and settling in services.

11. AFFORDABLE HOME OWNERSHIP AND HOME BUILDING SCHEMES – WHAT ARE THEY?

The government has designated financial assistance to help people buy or build homes who might otherwise find it tricky, such as first-time buyers, older or disabled people.

If you are considering this option, do your homework to make sure the information on the various schemes is still up to date. For example, you may have heard of the "Help to Buy" scheme, but this ended in England in 2023. It has been extended in Wales to September 2026.

Whilst any support in buying/building a house is usually welcomed there are naturally various criteria and hoops to jump through, and the more you understand them the better.

It is important to note that often schemes vary between England and Wales. Here is an overview of some of the current schemes. Some of them may only apply to social housing.

ENGLAND

First Homes Scheme

- Opportunity to buy the home for 30-50% less than its market value.

- Applies to first-time buyers of their only or main residence.

- Only applies to new built houses or houses that have previously been owned but were part of the First Homes Scheme initially and are now being marketed through an estate agent.

- Buyer must be able to get a mortgage for at least half the price of the home.

- Buyer's income collectively cannot be more than £80,000 a year before tax, or £90,000 if the house is in London.

- Councils may set particular local eligibility criteria. e.g. prioritising key workers.

- Contact developers or estate agents about any First Homes scheme houses they have available. They will also check your eligibility criteria, help you to complete the application and they'll submit your application to the local authority.

- Once you have bought your home, you no longer have to meet the eligibility criteria, e.g. if you took a higher paying job.

- You can rent the house out for up to 2 years usually, and you can rent a room out to someone if you're still living in it.

- Usually, you can only sell the property to someone who is eligible under the First Homes scheme criteria, and you would need to give them the same percentage discount you had when you bought it.

Lifetime ISA

- You must be over 18 but under 40 to open a Lifetime ISA.

- You can put in up to £4,000 each year until you're 50, and the government will add a 25% bonus to your savings up to a maximum of £1,000 per year, until you are 50, after which it will continue to earn interest.

- You can withdraw money from it if you are buying your first home up to the value of £450,000 with a mortgage, you are over 60 or if you have less than 12 months to live. If you wish to withdraw for any other reason, there will be a charge of 25% to recoup the government bonus.

Shared Ownership Scheme

- You buy a 10-75% share of a property and pay rent to a landlord on the rest, as well as usually paying monthly service charges towards, for example, maintenance of any communal areas, and ground rent (see Tip 57).

- You can buy more shares in your home in the future.

- Homes are offered by housing associations, local councils or other organisations. They will check your eligibility.

- All shared ownership homes are leasehold properties (see Tip 57).

- Household income cannot be more than £80,000 a year before tax, or £90,000 if the house is in London.

- You must not be able to afford all of the deposit and mortgage payments for a home that meets your needs.

- If you're aged 55 or over at the time of buying the home, you can buy up to a 75% share through the Older Persons Shared Ownership (OPSO) scheme. Once you own 75%, you will not pay rent on the rest.

- You can apply for a scheme called home ownership for people with a long-term disability (HOLD). For example, if you need a ground floor home.

- You will need to pay for repairs and maintenance no matter what share you own.

- You can sublet a room provided you also live in the house.

- Selling your shares has specific conditions. As with all these schemes, make sure you are fully aware of all of the details and scenarios before committing.

Right to Shared Ownership Scheme

- Means you have a right to buy a share of your home that you currently rent, and become a leaseholder (see Tip 57), for certain eligible homes.

- You pay rent to the landlord on the difference i.e. the share of the home you don't own, and usually a monthly service charge for communal areas (see Tip 33).

- Must have been your only/main home for 1 year, and you must have been a tenant of social of affordable housing for at least 3 years.

- Similar to the Shared Ownership Scheme you can buy between 10-75% of your home's market value and there are conditions around eligibility, fees, what you can do with the property and how you sell it.

Rent to Buy Scheme

- Properties are offered to rent at a discount of usually 20% below market value, so that you can save for a deposit to buy a home.

- Properties in London are covered by their own specific scheme called "London Living Rent".

- Must be employed, a first-time buyer, (or buying after a relationship breakdown), and able to pay the rent and save for a deposit at the same time.

- Only applies to properties in the scheme. The Shared Ownership Scheme Service allows you to search for the organisations who offer them.

- Initial tenancy is for 2 years and landlord may agree to extend if you still need more time to save for a deposit.

Help to Build Scheme - England

- Eligible applicants can receive a 25 year equity loan ranging from 5% to 20% of the total estimated land and build costs, (maximum of 40% in London). This loan is interest-free for the first five years.

- The estimated costs excluding VAT and a contingency sum, cannot be more than £600,000 if you're buying the land and building your home, (the build cannot be more than £400,000), and £400,000 if you're building on land you already own.

- You can only apply if you have a 5% deposit of the total and you're also able to get a self-build mortgage from a lender registered with the Help to Build scheme. You'll need the lender's mortgage offer to apply.

- The loan can be used to buy land and build a new home on it, or buy unused space above an existing building to build a flat.

- Can be used to convert commercial property to residential.

- Can be used to demolish an existing building and replace with new.

- Can **not** be used to build more than one home, upgrade a home or create a second home, i.e. you must live in it when it is built and sell any other home within 12 months.

WALES

Help to Buy – Wales Scheme (currently extended to continue until September 2026).

- Welsh Government provides "equity mortgages" to buyers of new-build homes through a participating builder.

- Maximum price of the home is £300,000.

- You must provide a 5% deposit, the scheme provides a 25 year equity mortgage on up to 20% of the purchase price and you take out a repayment mortgage, (i.e. not interest only), to cover the rest.

- You are not allowed to sub-let any part of the house.

- You are not allowed to be renting your existing home and buying a second home through the scheme.

- Changing ownership or making alterations to the property will require Welsh Government permission.

- The house needs to have a minimum EPC rating of B, (see Tip ??).

Lifetime ISA

- You must be over 18 but under 40 to open a Lifetime ISA.

- You can put in up to £4,000 each year until you're 50, and the government will add a 25% bonus to your savings up to a maximum of £1,000 per year, until you are 50, after which it will continue to earn interest.

- You can withdraw money from it if you are buying your first home up to the value of £450,000 with a mortgage, you are over 60 or if you have less than 12 months to live. If you wish to withdraw for any other reason, there will be a charge of 25% to recoup the government bonus.

Homebuy – Wales

- Welsh Government provide a 30% equity loan to assist with purchasing an existing property. Only available in certain areas bases on local eligibility criteria.

- You contribute 70% of purchase price through mortgage or savings, the loan against the property covers the remaining 30% but there are no monthly payments for it.

- You must repay 30% of the value of your property when you sell it to pay the loan of, or you can repay the loan beforehand.

- You must not be able to afford to buy a home that meets your needs.

- Homes are usually available through a Registered Social Landlord, (RSL).

Shared Ownership Scheme

- You buy a 25-75% share of a property and pay rent to a landlord on the rest, as well as any service charges (see Tip 33).

- You can buy more shares in your home in the future.

- You must take out a repayment mortgage for the share of the home you purchased i.e. not an interest only mortgage.

- Only applies to eligible homes from participating landlords.

- Household income cannot be more than £60,000 a year before tax.

- Applies to first-time buyers of their only or main residence or forming a new household e.g. after relationship breakup, or relocating for work to an area you can't afford.

- You must not be able to afford to buy a home that meets your needs.

- You are not allowed to sub-let any part of the house.

- You will need to pay for repairs and maintenance no matter what share you own.

- Selling your shares has specific conditions. As with all of these schemes, make sure you are fully aware of all of the details and scenarios before committing.

Rent to Own Scheme

- Tenants in eligible rented properties have the opportunity to build up a lump sum towards a deposit to buy their home whilst they are renting it.

- The agreement lasts up to five years and you can receive 25% of the rent paid during that time, and 50% of the increase in the property value (if any), during that time to use as a deposit towards buying it.

- You can apply to buy the house between the end of year 2 and year 5, (end), of the agreement.

- Household income cannot be more than £60,000 a year and you must be in work or self employed.

- You must not be eligible for housing benefit.

- You must not own another home, (with some exceptions), and you must be unable to afford to buy a home another way.

Self-Build Wales

- An initiative to help people build their own home in Wales is known as "Self Build Wales".

- It is a development loan for up to two years. Interest on the loan rolls up and is added to the balance of the loan monthly.

- There is usually no requirement to repay the loan until completion of the build. You will need to provide evidence of how you will pay it e.g. through a mortgage "Agreement in Principle".

- The scheme offers three routes to building your own home;

a. You can choose from one of their Self Build Wales "oven ready" building plots with planning permission already in place. In which case you can apply for 75% of the land purchase and 100% of the build costs.

b. You can build on land you already own subject to relevant statutory permissions and various conditions. In this case you can apply for up to 50% of the value of the land to make it ready for development and 100% of the building costs.

c. You can find your own land to buy provided it already has suitable planning permission. The scheme could support up to 75% of the land purchase and 100% of the build costs.

- Various conditions apply such as the costs to build the property are capped at £350,000, and arrangement fees and exit fees are payable.

- The builder will need to be TrustMark accredited. If you are a builder by trade and want to build the home yourself, you will still need to be TrustMark accredited.

- You will need to appoint a Contract Administrator for the works who is a recognised professional.

- You can't rent or sell the home for 5 years from completion.

12. SHOULD I BUY A FLAT/APARTMENT?

For some people buying a flat or apartment, (these words tend to get used interchangeably), is a choice made simply because it is what is most affordable to them in their location. For others it is a lifestyle choice that means they don't have individual responsibility for the various external maintenance tasks such as mowing the lawn or clearing out the gutters.

There are various reasons why you might want to buy a flat or apartment; weighing up the advantages and considerations can help you make a decision that is right for you.

Advantages

- They are generally more affordable than houses, especially in urban areas where property and land prices are high.

- You may find there is more availability of flats/apartments in cities, rather than houses, so you have more choice.

- Maintenance responsibilities are often less, as many flats come with management services for common areas.

- They are typically located in urban areas, close to amenities like shops, restaurants, and public transport.

- They often have additional security measures like gated entries, intercom systems, and communal security.

Considerations

Leasehold vs. Freehold (see Tips 57 and 58)

- Leasehold: Most flats are sold as leasehold, meaning you own the property but not the land it's on. Check the lease length and terms, as short leases can affect property value and mortgage availability. Also take note that legislation is changing in this respect, so it is worth familiarising yourself with the Leasehold and Freehold Reform Act 2024.

- Freehold: Less common for flats/apartments, but it would mean you own both the property and the land it sits in/on. Be aware that many lenders won't lend against freehold flats/apartments.

Service charges and ground rent

- Service charges are regular payments for the maintenance of communal areas, lifts, gardens, and sometimes amenities like gyms or pools (see Tip 33).

- Occasionally, depending on the terms of your agreement, you may also be served a Section 20 Notice which caters to additional charges for "major works". These are more legally complex and infrequent but can have big consequences. A well maintained and statutory compliant building both inside and out will help to avoid these. As always it is recommended you do your research and take professional advice in this respect.

- Ground rent applies to some leasehold properties. It is an annual payment to the freeholder for your right to occupy the land on which the property is built on.

- Ensure you understand these costs and how they might increase over time.

- It is worth noting the condition of the whole building and communal areas before buying, and not just the condition of your flat/apartment. Thid could give you an indication of how well maintained it is and whether more significant maintenance expenses are likely to arise in the near future.

Management company

- Investigate the management company responsible for maintaining the property and check out their reputation. Poor management can lead to high charges and inadequate upkeep.

- Understand if there is a reserve fund for major repairs to manage unexpected large payments.

Building Regulations and safety

- As with any building purchase it is important to check that the necessary statutory consents/compliance have been achieved, and if not develop a plan for whether you still want to/are able to buy the property and how it might affect you (see Tip 47).

- Post the Grenfell Tower fire in 2017, the safety of cladding on high-rise flats in particular has been a significant concern. Some mortgage lenders still require an EWS1 form (External Wall System form; a safety assessment introduced in 2019 to evaluate the fire risk associated with cladding on multi-occupancy residential buildings), for buildings over 18 metres high, or lower rise buildings which they deem to be higher risk. Understanding whether this applies to you early in your home buying journey could save you time and money.

- Ask to see the building's "Fire Risk Assessment" (a legally required document), and check the fire safety measures in place, including alarms, sprinklers, and fire exits.

- Ask to see the building's asbestos register and management plan. Whilst the duty to manage asbestos containing materials (ACMs) in communal areas will rest with the landlord/managing agent, planned works to these areas which involve ACMs could be more costly. This could ultimately affect the charges passed on to leaseholders.

Mortgages and financing

- Some lenders have restrictions on lending for flats, particularly those in high-rise buildings, with short leases or with freeholds. Identify these as soon as possible and ideally before you've spent on professional fees.

- Ensure you understand the total cost of ownership, including mortgage payments, service charges, ground rent, and maintenance costs. Make sure these are factored into your measure of affordability (see Tip 28).

Insurance

- Buildings insurance covers the structure of the building, including walls, roof, floors, and permanent fixtures. For leasehold flats, the freeholder usually arranges this, and the cost is included in the service charges. Check that this is in place and what it covers/excludes.

- Contents insurance covers personal belongings within the flat and is usually the responsibility of the person living there.

- For those renting out their flat, landlord insurance covers the risks associated with tenants and rental properties, which normal home insurance might not.

Amenities and community

- Some flats offer communal amenities like gyms, gardens, or roof terraces. These can enhance lifestyle but also often come with higher service charges.

- Consider the community vibe and whether the building has a good mix of residents that align with your lifestyle.

- Check for any restrictions which might affect your lifestyle such as any rules around keeping pets, having parties, sub-letting/Airbnb.

- See how the building aligns with your lifestyle and comfort; for example, you may be particularly sensitive to noise transfer between apartments and some buildings will be better than others in this respect; or you may feel uncomfortable if your front door is at the end or a poorly lit corridor.

13. SHOULD I BUY A NEW HOME?

There really are compelling arguments both for and against new homes. Again, the main factor to think about is those first principles; why are you buying a house in the first place? (see Tip 1). What sort of lifestyle do you want to have and how might a new home affect or support that? As an alternative you could also consider building your own new home, and there are government financial initiatives to help with this (see Tip 11).

Financial considerations

- As with any property purchase, create a budget and assess your financial situation, including savings, income, and any debts.

- Factor in additional costs such as stamp duty, legal fees, survey costs, moving expenses, and consider ongoing costs like council tax, utility bills, and maintenance.

- Determine how much you can afford for a deposit and monthly mortgage payments, also how much you can afford for ongoing monthly running costs and council tax.

- Get a mortgage agreement in principle to understand how much you can borrow and compare mortgage deals from various lenders to find the best terms.

- New housing developers may offer incentives like stamp duty contributions, upgraded fixtures, or help with legal fees. Evaluate these offers carefully in the context of your budget and keep a level head in deciding whether buying a new home is right for you.

Location

- Research the local area, including schools, transport links, amenities, and crime rates.

- Visit the area at different times of the day to get a sense of the environment.

- Research local planning development plans and records to understand if further development is likely to happen and how that might affect you.

- Speak to the developer about any ongoing building work in the surrounding area, how long this is likely to take and how you might be affected, e.g. by unfinished access roads, or frequent deliveries.

Property specifications

- Understand the quality of the new build; investigate the reputation of the developer. Ask about the specification of the building design and materials and research their quality and life expectancy.

- Check that the property comes with a warranty, such as the NHBC (National House Building Council) Buildmark warranty.

- Ask if there is an opportunity for you to request "variations" to the final specification, (if buying off plan), e.g. kitchen fittings.

- Space; how much space has been allocated to things like storage. Unlike a show home, you are actually going to be living in this house, which means unless you are a secret "KonMarie" ninja, you are going to need plenty of space for all life's things. (see Tip 24).

Energy efficiency

- New homes tend to have better energy efficiency because the standards to which they have had to be built continue to increase.

- Read the Energy Performance Certificate (EPC) and gain an initial understanding of what energy efficiency measures the building features.

- Look for features like quality window and doors, good insulation, and energy-efficient heating systems. Many of these are now statutory requirements, but the bar is always being raised.

- Buying a new home is a great opportunity to find a house that has been built with that bit extra in terms of energy efficiency, (rather than just the statutory requirement), to help future proof it for longer.

Legal and regulatory aspects

- Understand the difference between leasehold and freehold properties (see Tips 57 and 58).

- Most new-build houses are freehold, but new-build flats are often leasehold. Although keep an eye on the Leasehold and Freehold Reform Act 2024 for changes to this.

- There are also some new build private housing estates, where the seller/developer retains the freehold, (at least until they potentially sell it on), and new homeowners are required to pay leasehold charges such as ground rent (where essentially the ground is not your own), and communal area service charges.

- It is important to know as soon as possible what the legal position of the property is and whether any charges could apply, as well as understanding how this may change in the future, (e.g. when there are rent reviews), and/or potentially affect the re-sale value.

- Many leaseholds may require you to obtain the freeholder's consent e.g. for making alterations to a property or may restrict how you use your home.

- As with any building purchase it is important to check that the necessary statutory consents/compliance have been achieved.

- In particular ensure that all necessary planning permissions and building regulations approvals are satisfactorily discharged.

Inspection and surveys

- For new builds, consider a snagging survey to identify any defects or incomplete work.

- Ensure any serious issues are addressed by the developer before completion of the purchase.

- Check if there is a "defects liability period" and what this is, then make sure the remaining snags are boxed off before this time expires.

Contracts and warranties

- Have your solicitor review the contract thoroughly.

- Ensure you understand all terms and conditions, including any timeline for completion of the development and any penalties for delays.

- New builds usually come with warranties (e.g., NHBC, LABC). Check the duration and what is covered.

- Obtain copies of all completion documentation including architect's certificates or professional consultant's certificate to satisfy your mortgage lender, electrical and gas certificates, any Health and Safety or Operating and Maintenance Manuals which may be available with the property.

- It is also helpful to obtain a copy of the plans and specification of the building for the benefit of potential future alterations/maintenance.

Resale value and trends

- As with any property research the local property market to understand trends and prospects should you decide to re-sell or rent it out in future.

- Consider the long-term resale value of the property.

14. SHOULD I BUY "OFF PLAN"?

Buying a new home "off plan" involves purchasing a property before it has been completed, sometimes even before construction has started, when perhaps you have only seen the architect's plans and illustrations of it. This approach can have its advantages, but it also comes with unique risks and considerations.

Financial considerations

- Developers often offer discounts for off-plan purchases. Look for incentives like upgraded fixtures, payment of legal fees, or stamp duty contributions, and factor these into your overall budget and plans.

- Typically, you'll need to pay a deposit (often 10-20% of the purchase price) at the time of signing the contract.

- In some cases, you may need to make stage payments as construction progresses. Make sure whatever payments you make have been contractually agreed and executed in consultation with your solicitor.

Mortgage considerations

- Ensure your mortgage lender is aware you are buying off plan as soon as possible. Not all lenders are happy to lend on properties that are off plan so you may find there are fewer providers to choose from.

- Obtain a mortgage agreement in principle but ensure it remains valid until after the house build is completed, otherwise you may end up having to reapply.

- Some lenders might not issue a formal mortgage offer until the property is near completion.

- Negotiate as much breathing space as possible with your lender, in case construction works are delayed. Often mortgage offers are only valid for six months.

- Lenders will usually require a valuation of the completed property before releasing funds.

- Be aware that the property's value may change between the contractual exchange and completion date (see Tip 2). A "down valuation" would mean the completed property may be valued lower than the purchase price at exchange, which could affect mortgage availability and terms.

- Depending on timescales, in severe cases where mortgage lender offers have expired and a new offer could not be secured, (possibly due to a down valuation or a change in buyer circumstances/affordability), homeowners have been forced to pull out of the purchase and have faced losing deposits. In extreme cases they may even have had to pay developer penalties.

- Speak to your solicitor about agreeing a "long-stop completion date" with the developer that is before your mortgage offer expires. It is also worth researching local market trends to assess potential risks.

Legal and contractual aspects

- Hire a solicitor experienced in off-plan purchases to review the contract thoroughly.

- Understand all terms, including completion date, specification details, and what happens if the developer fails to complete on time (also refer to Tip 13).

Warranty and insurance

- Ensure the property comes with a warranty, such as one provided by NHBC, LABC Warranty, Checkmate and Premier Guarantee; and understand when this expires.

- As with any property, speak to insurers early on, letting them know you are buying off plan and find out what insurance options are available to you and what you need to do when.

- Consumer Code for Home Builders; applies to most new build homes covered by one of the big warranty providers. Check the developer adheres to it.

- Check if the developer is a member of a redress scheme to handle potential disputes.

Developer reputation and build quality

- Investigate the developer's track record for quality and reliability. Look at past projects and customer reviews.

- Ensure the developer is financially stable to complete the project. Ask your solicitor about carrying out a credit check on them to gain a fuller picture.

- Ensure the contract details all specifications, including materials and finishes. Verify what is included in the purchase price, and that you are happy with the quality of items specified.

- Plan for a snagging survey before completion to identify any defects or incomplete work (see Tip 3).

Timing and flexibility

- Be prepared for potential delays. Understand the contractual terms regarding completion date extensions and penalties for late completion.

- Be prepared to arrange temporary accommodation and storage if there are delays, particularly if you are selling your current home (see Tip 24).

- Consider how well the property will meet your future needs in terms of size, layout, and location.

Practical tips

- If possible, visit a show home to get an idea of what the finished property will look like.

- Study the floor plans and site plans carefully to understand the layout and orientation of the property.

- As with any property consider the potential resale value and how easy it will be to sell the property in the future.

- If you plan to rent out the property, research the local rental market to ensure it's a viable investment. Also check the legal documents for the property to understand any planning or mortgage stipulations which could affect when and how you rent your property, particularly for short term/holiday lets.

15. SHOULD I BUY A RENOVATION PROJECT?

Buying a house that needs renovating can be both exciting and stressful.

If you buy the property at the right price and can keep a reign on renovations costs, then these projects can be a potentially rewarding investment that also allow you to put your own mark on a place. But it's not for everyone. Renovating comes with risks and challenges both from a financial and personal perspective. There's a lot to be said for moving straight into a house that doesn't need anything doing to it. Depending on what you want out of life will help you decide if a renovation project is right for you now (see Tip 1).

Pros of buying a renovation project

- Properties needing renovation are often priced below market value, providing an opportunity to buy in a desirable area at a lower cost.

- It allows you to customise the property to your taste and needs and gives you the pleasure of exercising your creative genius.

- Well thought out and properly executed renovations can significantly increase the property's market value, leading to a potential profit upon resale.

- Potentially fewer buyers are willing to take on renovation projects, which can reduce competition and make it easier to negotiate a good price.

- If it's a significant renovation project, or conversion, mainstream mortgage lending may not be an option – this could reduce the amount of people competing to buy the property and potentially reduce the price.

Cons of buying a renovation project

- Renovations often come with unforeseen expenses due to hidden issues like structural problems, outdated wiring, or plumbing.

- They can take longer than expected, often due to unforeseen issues or complexities in adding retrofit solutions. This can cause delays in moving in or reselling and can add to costs.

- Managing a renovation project can be stressful and requires time and effort to oversee project professionals, contractors and ensure quality work.

- Maintaining clear communication between the project team and managing your expectations vs contractor's commitment/availability can be frustrating.

- If you are undertaking some work yourself it can be difficult and tiring to juggle work, family and social lives all whilst learning and applying new skills. It can also be physically demanding.

- Securing a mortgage for a property that needs significant work can be challenging, and lenders may require a higher deposit or interest rate. Your choice of lenders could be significantly reduced or not available at all.

- Depending on the property, (e.g. if it is listed see Tip 61), and the extent of renovation works being carried out, you may need statutory consents such as Planning Permission or Building Regulation approval. It would be sensible to take professional advice to understand what consents will be necessary, what will be involved in obtaining them, and whether any particular requirements need fulfilling e.g. by your lender or by the planning authority.

Other considerations

- Ensure the renovations align with local market demands to maximise the property's resale value. For example, it probably wouldn't be worth creating a "Barbie dream house" in an area where 2-bedroom apartments for retirees are what is wanted.

- Insuring a property under renovation can be more expensive and complex. Consider specialised renovation insurance.

- Certain renovations may be eligible for reduced VAT rates e.g. if the house hasn't been lived in for 2 years or more then most of the work may be charged at a reduced VAT rate of 5%.

- If the renovation is your only home and you've lived in it as your main home for all the time you've owned it, and you haven't bought it just to make a gain, then you may be entitled to "Private Residence Relief" which means you wouldn't have to pay Capital Gains Tax (CGT) when you eventually sell the house on any profit you may have made in renovating it. However, speak to a tax specialist to make sure you know any liability you are likely to encounter, before buying the property.

- If you are planning on living in the property whilst you are renovating it be aware that there may be times when it is not safe to occupy, or you could be without basic services such as water or power.

16. SHOULD I BUY A TINY HOME?

A "tiny home" in the UK is typically a small, compact house that is designed to maximise space and efficiency. These homes are often under 400 square feet and can be mobile (built on trailers) or fixed on foundations. Tiny homes typically appeal to those seeking a minimalist lifestyle, lower living costs, and a reduced environmental footprint.

Tiny homes are gaining traction in the UK, particularly amongst young people who for example after university would rather not live with their parents, (or have parents who would rather their kids didn't move back in!), and who don't want to be living in a house share or breaking the bank on paying rent. A tiny home can give them the autonomy of owning their own house, but with more financial freedom and less time commitment.

Statutory and legal considerations

This is usually the biggest obstacle for people wanting to live in a tiny home. It is not uncommon for buyers to get "creative" with their interpretation of the respective rules and regulations for their areas, but Local Authorities are becoming increasingly aware of these, and there are risks of repercussions.

- For stationary tiny homes, you may need planning permission depending on local council regulations, the exact placement of your tiny home e.g. within a "curtilage", and how you intend to occupy it. Check with your local planning authority or speak to a local Planning Consultant.

- Mobile tiny homes with wheels might be considered caravans under the law, but long-term placement or occupation could still require planning consent.

- Mobile tiny homes with wheels may be exempt from some building regulations if they are classified as caravans under the law, but they will still need to meet certain design and safety criteria for construction.

- Stationary tiny homes must comply with building regulations, which cover structural safety, insulation, and fire safety.

- Ensure you have legal rights to place your tiny home on the chosen land, whether you own it or rent it.

- Verify the land use designation (planning permission use class) and any restrictions on the type of dwelling allowed.

Home Buyer's Essentials

Financial considerations

- Tiny homes can be more affordable than traditional houses, typically ranging from £20,000 to £100,000 depending on size, materials, and customisation.

- Securing a mortgage for a tiny home can be challenging. Personal loans or self-financing are common alternatives.

- Utility bills and maintenance costs are generally lower due to the smaller size and energy-efficient design of tiny homes.

- Insurance might be different from standard home insurance, especially for mobile tiny homes.

- Consider the potential resale value and market demand for tiny homes in your area. They may not appreciate in value like traditional homes. It is also crucial that you have the correct statutory consents in place in order to realise the resale value potential.

Practical considerations

- Is the site where you want to place your tiny home connected to adequate utilities, e.g electric, water, drainage, or is it an "off grid" project – in which case how will utilities be designed/installed and how reliable will they be?

- Will you have your own postal address?

- Efficient use of space is crucial. Furniture is often multi-functional (e.g., foldable tables, sofa beds), and storage solutions are maximised.

- Living in a tiny home requires a minimalist approach, with a focus on reducing belongings and simplifying lifestyle.

- If the tiny home is on wheels, consider how often you plan to move, and the logistics involved in relocating.

17. HOW DO I BUY FROM AN AUCTION?

Auctions are often packed with renovation projects (see Tip 15), and you can sometimes bag a property that wouldn't have been affordable via the more traditional type of open market.

I love a property auction, in fact I just love auctions in general, since they appeal to my love of uncertainty. But consider that for a moment, when buying a house at auction you will usually face a good deal of uncertainty. It is important not to get too emotionally invested in the house you're buying (as is always sensible with property if you can manage it), because doing so could mean you get swept away in auction fever and overstretch your budget. Alternatively, you could be bitterly disappointed if you do miss out on the home of your dreams.

At an auction the buyers in the room (or virtual room), are usually those who have relatively easy access to funds, because they are obliged to complete on the purchase typically within 2-6 weeks. When they buy a property at auction, they often are required to put down a 10% deposit straight away, as well as any associated costs, and if they don't meet the completion deadline, they lose this. Clearly the buying style is not conducive with traditional mortgage lending, which can be uncertain and lengthy; that's not to say you can't buy at auction with a mortgage, but the style of purchase is frankly better suited to cash "esque" buyers. What all this means is that you typically have a much smaller pool of potential buyers than you would on the open market, which could also work in your favour.

Auction houses have, like the rest of the world, endeavoured to keep up with technology and so now attract buyers from telephone and online audiences too – in fact more commonly the auctions themselves are held entirely online as opposed to in a single room.

Pre-auction preparation

Research and identify properties

- Obtain auction catalogues from auction houses and online auction platforms. These provide details of the properties available.

- Attend viewings for properties of interest to assess their condition and potential, as well as the local area.

- Check the small print with the conditions of the sale and familiarise yourself with any fees, timings or other clauses. Don't underestimate the importance of this.

- Ask the auction house to keep you informed of any alterations to the sale conditions, sometimes known as an "Addendum".

- Ask about the possibility of the house being sold to you before the auction date – sometimes this will be considered.

Legal checks

- Obtain and review the legal pack for the property. This includes title deeds, local authority searches, and special conditions of sale.

- Engage a solicitor to review the legal pack and advise on any legal issues.

- Legal packs can be released close to the auction date itself, so be prepared to act fast once you have it.

- Ensure that any existing alterations or extensions to the house have the necessary planning permissions and building regulation approvals (see Tips 47 and 49).

- Get your ID ready. Check what the auction house require; for many they will require two forms of ID on the auction day.

Financing

- If you need a mortgage, secure an agreement in principle. Ensure your lender is aware you are buying at auction, as funds need to be available quickly.

- Check that the property is mortgageable (see Tip 18). If the property needs work, it may be that the mortgage company won't lend until that work is done.

- Ensure that your mortgage provider can release funds within the completion period. Bridging finance may be necessary if there are delays, but this can be especially expensive, and the risks should be fully understood before committing to it.

- Arrange for the deposit, typically 10% of the purchase price, which is payable on the auction day.

- Ensure you are aware of, and budget for, all the fees associated to the purchase including those from the auction house itself, (such as buyer's fees usually 1-2%), tax and professional fees such as solicitors and surveyors. Make sure you know when these fees will need paying and how (see Tip 27).

- If the property is run down, make sure you have factored in renovation costs and time to your overall budget. If you are planning on eventually selling the property, make sure you have factored in any Capital Gains Tax which may be applicable.

- Research auction bidding strategies and decide how you are going to bid ahead of auction day – yes, these things do get tactical.

- If you haven't bought in an online auction before, practise your auction experience by buying something of low value but with several bids on it, on eBay for example. You'll be surprised at what you'll learn from the experience.

- Generally, residential property transactions are exempt from VAT, but certain conditions might apply, especially for commercial properties or mixed-use developments. Make sure this is confirmed.

Valuation and surveys

- Consider getting an independent valuation to ensure the property is worth the price you are willing to pay.

- Conduct any necessary surveys (see Tip 3), to identify potential building issues.

- Make sure the surveyors are aware of the auction date and any deadlines you need to meet beforehand to make sure you are ready for auction day.

Auction day

In-person auctions

- Register with the auction house, usually in advance, but may be on the day.

- Attend the auction and bid on your chosen property. Ensure you set a maximum bid limit and stick to it.

- If your bid is successful, you will need to pay the deposit immediately and sign the contract of sale.

Online auctions

- Register on the online auction platform and verify your identity – do this as early as possible before the auction.

- Make sure you are bidding from somewhere with a reliable and quick internet connection. There are few things more frustrating than the connection buffering as the auction clock counts down.

- Place bids online within the specified auction period. Online auctions can run for several days.

- If successful, follow the platform's instructions for paying the deposit and completing the necessary paperwork.

Post-auction process

Completion

- Completion usually takes place within 28 days from the auction date, though this can vary from 2-6 weeks. Ensure you have the remaining funds available to pay in this time.

- Transfer the remaining balance to the seller's solicitor to complete the purchase.

- Your solicitor will register the property transfer with the Land Registry, making you the official owner.

- Properties sold at auction are typically sold 'as seen'. It's crucial to understand that you have limited recourse for issues discovered after purchase.

18. WHAT IF THE HOUSE IS "UNMORTGAGEABLE" ?

If you need a mortgage to buy a house, and your lender refuses because the house is "unmortgageable", it is important to bear in mind that not all lenders will have the same lending criteria. Try contacting other mortgage lenders or speak to a mortgage broker, before deciding whether you can, and want to, continue with the purchase.

Unmortgageable properties could fall short of various criteria set by mortgage lenders, including structural issues, legal complications, or location problems. They are deemed unmortgageable because lenders consider them too risky to finance with a mortgage.

If you don't need a mortgage, buying an "unmortgageable" house can be a challenging yet potentially rewarding investment… if you know what you are doing. There is often less competition from other buyers for the property and you may be able to buy the property cheaper than if it was mortgageable.

Being unmortgageable doesn't necessarily mean the house will never pass a mortgage lender's criteria if it is improved, but it may mean that most mainstream mortgage lenders won't offer a mortgage based on how it is currently.

Possible reasons for unmortgageability

- Structural problems: significant issues like subsidence, severe water ingress, or structural damage.

- Non-standard construction: properties built with unconventional materials or methods e.g. some prefabricated homes.

- Legal issues: complications such as missing or defective title deeds, planning permissions or legal disputes.

- Short-leases: if it's a leasehold property (see Tip 57), typically those with less than 80 years remaining on the lease can struggle to obtain a mortgage, or if they do may struggle to obtain favourable terms.

- Location: properties located in areas with high likelihood of flooding, near hazardous sites, or on land with legal restrictions.

- Condition: properties in a serious state of disrepair, or those without essential amenities (e.g., no kitchen or bathroom).

Financing options

- Cash purchase: this is the most straightforward method to buy the house if you can secure the available funds. Needless to say, the seller won't be expecting you to turn up with briefcases full of cash – red flag if they do. A simple bank transfer will usually suffice. Be aware that money laundering legislation will require scrutiny of where the funds have come from.

- Bridging loans: short-term loans designed to cover the cost of the property until longer-term financing can be arranged or the property is sold. This can be expensive and risky. Seriously do your homework before committing to this.

- Renovation mortgages: some lenders offer products that combine the purchase and renovation costs, but these are less common and often come with stringent conditions.

Costs and risks

- Assess and document the full scope of renovation work required and obtain detailed quotes from contractors and professionals.

- Allow some budget for unforeseen issues that might arise during renovation. The construction industry is a fan of adding 10% of the known costs as a contingency sum, but if you suspect there could be more significant unknown risks, it would make sense to budget more.

- Insurance: obtaining insurance for an unmortgageable property can be more complex and expensive.

- Take professional advice from Chartered Surveyors and Solicitors.

Statutory consents

- Planning permission: check whether any planned renovations require planning permission.

- Building regulations: ensure all works comply with building regulations to avoid future legal issues.

- Check what other statutory consents/certificates may be required either from regulatory bodies or your lender, for example listed building consent or EWS1 forms (see Tip12).

19. HOW DO I BUY A BUY TO LET?

You may be buying a house with the intention of letting/renting it out, (these words are used interchangeably), to tenants.

Purchasing a buy-to-let property involves specific steps and considerations, including financial planning, understanding legal obligations, and ongoing management.

Financial planning

- Most lenders offer specific buy-to-let mortgages which typically require a higher deposit, (usually 20% or more), and have different lending criteria compared to residential mortgages.

- You can be in breach of contract if you don't have the right mortgage for your circumstances, or if you don't let your mortgage lender know if circumstances change, so make sure you know where you stand. A good mortgage broker can advise you.

- Interest rates on buy-to-let mortgages can be higher than those on residential mortgages, it is worth shopping around or using the services of a mortgage broker.

- Buy-to-let mortgages are usually offered on an interest only repayment basis, so it's important you have a plan for repayment of the mortgage capital at the end of the term.

- Lenders will assess the potential rental income to ensure it covers the mortgage payments. This is called interest cover ratios, (ICR). They use various methods, but often the rental income needs to be 125-145% of the mortgage interest.

- Initial fees for buy-to-let mortgages tend to be much higher so be sure to factor these in.

- If you have four or more buy-to-let properties you will often be described as a "portfolio" landlord, a distinction which means there could be more stringent rules to access finance.

- Buy-to-let properties incur different stamp duty thresholds and rates, make sure you factor these in.

- Tax changes has meant more landlords have set up company structures for their buy-to-let portfolios. Be aware however that this can mean you paying higher interest rates for your mortgage so be sure get specialist advice before deciding the best route for you.

- As with any purchase be sure to factor in solicitor or conveyancer fees for handling the legal aspects of the purchase, as well as any property surveys.

- Budget for any necessary renovations or furnishings to make the property tenant-ready. Tenant ready also means being statutory compliant in respect of renting. You may need to upgrade various parts of the building e.g. fire prevention, EPC rating (see Tip 20).

Location

- Choose areas with high rental demand, such as those near universities, transport links, and employment centres.

- Calculate the rental yield to ensure the investment is worthwhile. Yield = (annual rental income / property price) x 100. Generally, a gross rental yield of more than 5% is considered reasonable.

- Consider the long-term capital growth potential of the area.

Property type

- Consider your target tenant market (e.g., students, families, young professionals) and choose a property type that suits their needs.

- Assess the property's condition and the amount of work needed to make it rentable.

Licensing

- If you are buying a house in multiple occupation (HMO), check if a licence is required. Usually if you have 5 or more people from at least two separate households living together with shared facilities you will need one.

- HMOs typically need additional safety measures and adherence to specific regulations.

- Be aware that if you have had to obtain planning permission to convert a house to a HMO this is different to licensing and you are likely to require both.

Tenancy agreements

- In England ASTs (Assured Shorthold Tenancy), are still the most common type of tenancy agreement for homes, typically lasting a minimum of 6 or 12 months. These are set to change in 2025 to periodic tenancies with no fixed term and it is expected that the changes will apply to both new and existing tenancy agreements.

- In Wales all ASTs were changed to Standard Occupation Contracts in December 2022, which could either be fixed term, (i.e. with an end date agreed), or periodic contracts, (i.e. contract continues to roll forward).

- There is a roll out of reforms taking place affecting the legal rights of domestic Landlords and Tenants. In Wales the Renting Homes Wales Act 2016 presented a big shift and in England the Renters (Reform) Bill 2024, which is expected to become law in 2025, will have significant implications. It is important to understand both these and other Landlord and Tenant legislation before committing to buying a buy-to-let.

- It's sensible to obtain legal advice to draft tenancy agreements and ensure compliance with landlord-tenant laws.

Insurance

- Landlord insurance can cover property damage, loss of rent, and liability claims. It's essential for protecting your investment. Make sure you do your research and are clear on any requirements and coverage.

Ongoing management

- Handling tenant issues, maintenance, and compliance yourself can save money but requires more time and effort than you might expect. Be sure to factor this in.

- Hiring a letting agent to manage the property can be convenient but comes at a cost (typically 7-12% of rental income).

- It is important to budget for and undertake regular maintenance to ensure the property remains in good condition and complies with safety regulations. A simple planned maintenance survey and programme of works can help you plan for the longer term and reduce the likelihood of more serious defects or breakdowns which are disruptive to both you and the tenant.

- Budget for unexpected, (reactive), repairs and maintenance issues.

Tax implications

- Buy to let properties are usually subject to higher rates of stamp duty. They may be less if you are a first-time house buyer, but in either case, make sure you are certain of what you will need to budget for before you commit to purchase.

- Depending on how you have bought and own the property rental income could be subject to income tax. Some landlords may set up a limited company to help mitigate this. Speak to a tax advisor to create the best strategy for you.

- Allowable expenses could include mortgage interest (subject to restrictions), letting agent fees, maintenance and repair costs.

- Capital gains tax could be payable on the profit made from selling the property.

- In all cases, it is worth seeking independent tax advice before buying the property to understand the best way to purchase and own the house for your particular circumstances.

20. WHAT IF THE HOUSE I'M BUYING ALREADY HAS TENANTS?

Needless to say, it is vitally important to confirm in writing exactly what the arrangements are in relation to existing tenants. This should include obtaining evidence of any existing tenancy agreements, licenses or any other correspondence or documentation which you will inherit. Your solicitor will need to scrutinise these and advise you of your responsibilities/risks. As a sensible buyer it would also be wise for you to familiarise yourself with the documents and their implications.

If you are buying the house with "vacant possession", you can't exchange contracts until the tenant has moved out. Make sure you find when they were served notice to vacate the property and that the expiration of their rental agreement ties in with your purchase timeline. Be sure to view the property once the tenant has moved out to make sure there is no damage or possessions left behind which you will want the landlord to address.

Depending on what you want from the property, e.g. a home or purely an investment, will affect what any existing tenancy agreements will mean to your plans.

Points to note if you are buying a house with a tenant in-situ

- Determine the type of tenancy agreement in place (e.g. Assured Shorthold Tenancy, Standard Occupation Contract etc). Review the terms and conditions, including the duration of the tenancy, rent amount, and any clauses related to termination.

- The tenancy agreement transfers to you upon completion of the purchase. The tenants have the right to stay until the end of their tenancy period.

- Tenants must be provided with your contact details using a Section 48 notice, informing them of the new landlord's address for rent payment and correspondence.

- Section 3 notice must be given to the tenants within two months of becoming the new landlord, detailing the change of ownership.

- Due diligence enquiries into the tenants, including rental payment history and any ongoing issues.

- Inspect the property to understand its condition and any immediate maintenance needs. Make sure it is statutory compliant and that you have copies of all certification and documentation required for a rental property, e.g. valid gas and electrical certificates, EPCs etc (see Tip 51).

- Arrange a meeting with the tenants post purchase to introduce yourself and discuss any concerns or questions they may have.

- Ensure the current rent covers your mortgage and other costs. Compare with local rental rates to assess if the rent is fair.

- Ensure the tenant's deposit is transferred to you and is held in a government-approved Tenancy Deposit Scheme.

- If the property will have tenants at the time of purchase, you may need a buy-to-let mortgage rather than a residential mortgage (see Tip 19).

- Update or obtain landlord insurance to cover the property and any rental-related risks.

- You can only evict tenants under certain conditions, following the legal procedures for eviction. Recent legislation has changed things significantly in this respect and you need to be sure on how this might affect your ownership. The National Residential Landlord's Association (NRLA) and other landlord organisations can give you a steer on this, as well as your solicitor.

- Higher rates of Stamp Duty Land Tax (SDLT)/Land Transaction Tax may apply. Be clear on this and budget for it.

- Rental income is subject to income tax (see Tip 19). Gain specific tax advice and keep detailed records of all rental income and allowable expenses for your tax return.

- If you sell the property in the future, Capital Gains Tax may be payable on any profit made from the sale.

21. HOW TO BUY WITH FAMILY/FRIENDS?

Buying a house with family or friends, can be a mutually beneficial way to get the home that you want. However, don't fall into the trap of believing that because you get on great in all other aspects of your lives, you will be fine when it comes to agreeing the infinitely tedious, but potentially life altering details, of home ownership and admin.

Speaking from experience.... twice....it pays dividends if you can draw up a list of "what happens ifs..." before you commit to buying the place, when you are both at your most amenable. That way when inevitable hurdles come your way, you both at least have a degree of knowing where you stand.

Establish clear agreements

- Decide whether you'll own the property as joint tenants or tenants in common:

    a. Joint tenants - Each person owns the property equally. If one person dies, their share automatically passes to the other owner(s).

    b. Tenants in common - Each person owns a specific share of the property, which can be unequal. Shares can be passed on to someone else through a will.

- Draft a Deed of Trust (or Declaration of Trust) to outline each person's share in the property, contributions towards the purchase price, mortgage payments, and other financial obligations. This legal document can help prevent disputes in the future.

- Agree on what will happen if one person wants to sell their share or move out. This should include how the property will be valued, whether others will have the first option to buy the share, and how any proceeds will be divided.

Financial considerations

- If you're applying for a joint mortgage, all parties will be equally responsible for the entire mortgage debt, not just their share. Lenders will assess the combined income and credit histories, so any financial issues from one person could affect the entire group's ability to secure a mortgage.

- Ensure that everyone involved is comfortable with the mortgage payments and that there's a contingency plan if someone's financial situation changes.

- Agree on how you'll split upfront costs like the deposit, legal fees, survey fees, stamp duty, and any renovations or repairs.

- Clarify who will be responsible for ongoing costs such as utilities, council tax, insurance, and maintenance. Consider setting up some form of joint account to manage these expenses.

Legal and practical considerations

- Each party should seek independent legal advice to understand their rights and obligations fully. This ensures that everyone's interests are protected, especially in complex situations.

- Ensure the property is adequately insured. If you're buying as joint tenants, a joint policy might be appropriate. If buying as tenants in common, you might need separate policies or a clear agreement on how premiums will be paid.

- Decide how and where you will hold legal and maintenance documentation relating to the property and ensure that you can all access these freely.

Communication and decision-making

- Maintain regular communication about the property, finances, and any issues that arise. Regular meetings, even informally in the pub, can help keep everyone on the same page and address concerns promptly.

- Agree on a decision-making process, particularly for significant decisions such as selling the property or making large improvements. This could involve unanimous agreement or a majority vote, depending on the ownership structure.

- Agree who is going to take responsibility for managing which aspects, e.g. resentment will soon settle in if all admin responsibilities fall to one person by default.

Exit strategy

- Decide in advance how you'll handle the sale of the property if the group decides to sell. This includes choosing an estate agent, setting a price, and dividing the proceeds.

- Agree on how the property will be valued if one person wants to sell their share. This could be done by an independent valuer to ensure fairness.

- Discuss and agree various scenarios which could arise e.g. one person meets a new partner and wants to move them into the house or add them to the mortgage; or one person wants to sell but the other person doesn't want to move and can't afford to buy them out.

22. HOW TO BUY FOR A FAMILY MEMBER?

Buying a house for a family member can be a generous and thoughtful gesture, but it comes with significant legal, financial, and tax implications. Some things to consider are highlighted below, but in all instances speak to legal, accounting and tax professionals first to help decide the best outcome for all parties.

Define the relationship and terms

- Decide whether the house will be a gift or if it will involve some form of loan or shared ownership. If it's a gift, the family member will own the property outright. If it's a loan, ensure the terms are clearly defined, including repayment terms and what happens if the family member defaults or circumstances change.

- You might consider joint ownership if you want to retain some control or share the investment. This could be structured as joint tenants or tenants in common (see Tip 21).

- If you're not gifting the property outright, a Deed of Trust can outline each party's financial contributions, responsibilities, and what happens if the property is sold or if circumstances change.

- If the family member is unable to manage the property themselves due to age or disability, a Power of Attorney arrangement may allow you to help manage their affairs. Speak to a specialist before making any decisions.

Financial considerations

- If you can buy the house outright, it simplifies the process. However, if a mortgage is involved, consider how it will be structured and whether the family member will contribute to payments.

- If the family member takes on the mortgage, you could help with the deposit or agree to pay part of the mortgage. Ensure this is legally documented.

- Clarify who will be responsible for ongoing costs like maintenance, repairs, utilities, and council tax. If you will be covering these, ensure you budget accordingly.

- Depending on the value of the property and whether it's an additional property for you, higher stamp duty rates might apply. If you are gifting the property, there might be stamp duty implications depending on the structure of the gift.

- If you sell the property later, you might be liable for Capital Gains Tax on any increase in value. This doesn't necessarily apply if the property was the primary residence of the person receiving the gift, but it could if you retain ownership and sell it later.

- Gifting a property could have inheritance tax implications. If you die within seven years of making the gift (currently being discussed that this may change), the value of the property may be included in your estate for inheritance tax purposes.

- Some people choose to put their property into trust for certain circumstances.

Legal and practical considerations

- Ensure that the title deeds are correctly transferred to the family member if the property is being gifted. This should be done through a solicitor to ensure the process is legally binding.

- If you want to retain some rights over the property (e.g., if you plan to live there as well), you could consider including a "right to reside" clause in the legal documents.

- Consider what will happen if circumstances change, such as the family member wanting to sell the property or if they face financial difficulties.

- Like "exit strategy" in Tip 21, it is worth having an open an honest conversation about all the "what ifs" and agree how you would navigate these before they potentially happen and the conversation inevitably becomes a lot harder.

Communication and family dynamics

- Discuss expectations openly with the family member to avoid misunderstandings. This could include scenarios like whether you are expecting any benefit in kind in return, such as care giving for dependents, or discussing what happens if the family member needs to temporarily relocate for works and wants to rent the property.

- It's wise to discuss the arrangement with other family members to prevent future disputes, especially if the property is being gifted as part of inheritance planning. Even the best family bonds can start to crack if people feel there has been favouritism or unfairness, (no matter how well intended!).

Seek professional advice

- Engage a solicitor to guide you through the process, ensuring that all legal documents are correctly drafted and that your interests are protected and those of the beneficiary.

- Consult a financial advisor with experience in estate planning to understand the full tax implications and to plan effectively, particularly regarding inheritance and capital gains tax.

- A financial advisor can help you plan how this purchase fits into your broader financial goals and obligations.

23. HOW DO I ORGANISE THE MOVE?

You will reach a point in your home buying journey where you will start to get the impression that the purchase is going to be successful. A little self-preservation tip, (and this may be too late to say it), but don't start daydreaming of your new life in your new home just yet as anything could happen; stay focussed on driving the purchase through to completion when you have those keys in your hand.

Having said that if you are moving into the property this is usually the time people start packing. If you can avoid becoming too excited about your new home, there is something to be said for starting to plan for the move even earlier; because if this property doesn't work out, there may be another one at some point. The more prepared to move you are the more flexible you can be, and the more likely you are to drive the purchase process forward and make it happen.

Organising a house move can be a complex and time-consuming process, but with careful planning, you can make it more manageable.

Create a moving plan and timeline

6-8 weeks before moving

- Declutter! Go through your belongings and decide what to keep/store, donate, sell, or discard. This reduces the amount you need to move and can even make the moving process cheaper.

- Make a detailed list of everything you plan to move. This will help you keep track of your belongings and ensure nothing is lost during the move.

- Decide how you are going to move. Will you use a removal company or are you planning on hiring a van? Will friends and family help you? Remember if you are in a chain (see Tip 26), you might only receive the keys for your new home on exactly the same day as you hand over the keys to your current home. Meaning either all your things will need to go straight from home A to home B in the space of several hours, or you will need to find somewhere to store them in the meantime.

- Where will you get boxes from? If you are planning to use recycled boxes you'll need to start collecting them, but make sure they are strong. If you are going to buy boxes you may want to shop around for the best value and quality. If you are using a removals company they may be able to include boxes in their price and are likely to prefer using their own which they know are up to the job.

4-8 weeks before moving

- If you are using a removals service research and book a reputable removal company. Get quotes from multiple companies to compare prices and services. Ensure the company is insured and has good reviews.

- If you are planning on hiring a van, research and book van hire and make sure you will have all the right insurances and licenses necessary for when you collect it; you don't want complications when you go to pick it up on moving day. Also be aware of any extra charges such as additional insurance costs; decisions should be kept to a minimum on moving day to limit stress.

- Begin packing items you don't use daily, such as out-of-season clothes, books, and decorative items. Label boxes clearly with their contents and the room they belong to in the new house.

2-4 weeks before moving

- Inform relevant parties of your change of address, including banks, utility companies, insurance providers, and the DVLA. Don't forget to redirect your mail through the Royal Mail's redirection service.

- Confirm the moving date, time, and any special requirements with the removal company. Ensure they have access to both your current and new properties.

- Speak to your solicitor to clarify key hand over arrangements and timescales.

Packing and organising

- Purchase or gather packing materials such as boxes, bubble wrap, packing tape, and markers. Consider wardrobe boxes for clothes, and special boxes for fragile items.

- Pack one room at a time to stay organised. Start with the least used rooms and work your way to the most used rooms.

- Label very clearly any boxes containing fragile items.

- Be sure not to overload boxes so they don't collapse on moving day and items get damaged.

- Clearly label each box with its contents and the room it should go to in the new house. This will make unpacking much easier.

- Pack an "Essentials Box"; include items you'll need immediately upon arrival, such as toiletries, a change of clothes, important documents, phone chargers, a kettle and cups, and bedding.

- Keep important documents (e.g., passports, contracts, birth certificates) in a separate, clearly marked folder and transport them yourself.

Moving day logistics

- Congratulations, the big day is here. First things first, breathe, make yourself a brew and take a moment to be present and appreciate your current home for one last time. A little self-care first thing in the morning can set you in the right direction for the rest of the day.

- If you are near to a takeaway, consider ordering in some breakfast for you and your moving crew. An army can't march on an empty stomach as they say, and you need everyone to pull together today.

- It might be helpful to have a crate of bottled water to hand and a few snacks. You and your helpers will need to stay refreshed, and it will save you money and time from running to the nearest coffee shop.

- Make sure any key swapping arrangements have been honoured or are going to plan.

- Make time to review any checklists you have, to make sure you feel comfortable and in control.

- If you have young children and pets, you may find it easier to arrange care for them so you can focus on the task at hand. But be sure to make the time to celebrate and ease them into the new house when they arrive, as it's a big thing for them to move home too.

- If you have arranged van hire collect the van, or if you are relying on an army of family and friends, perhaps set up a chat group to make sure everyone is turning up when planned, they know what they are doing, and any questions are answered promptly.

- If you are using a removals company, be present to oversee the team and answer any questions.

- Before leaving, do a final walkthrough of your old home to make sure nothing is left behind.

- At the new home guide people on where to place each box and piece of furniture. It helps to label rooms in the new house to match the labels on the boxes.

- If you haven't already, ensure that utilities such as gas, electricity, water, and internet are up and running in the new house.

- Start by unpacking your essentials box so you can quickly settle in. Then, move on to the kitchen and bedrooms.

- Remember to eat, stay hydrated, and take lots of photos to look back on. The day could feel exciting, or it could feel stressful. Just remember either way you will soon be settled in and enjoying your new home.

Post-move considerations

- If you haven't already you may want to change the locks on the doors of your new home. The previous owners may have been friendly, but you really don't know who else might have a key to what is now your property.

- Some people like to change the toilet seats in their new home. You can get their point! While the rooms are bare it is also a great opportunity to freshen the house up with a lick of paint.

- Unpack one room at a time, starting with the most essential areas such as the kitchen, bathroom, and bedrooms.

- If you haven't already, update your address with any services or subscriptions, including electoral roll registration.

- Introduce yourself to your new neighbours to start building a positive relationship in your new community. Some people exchange small gifts with new neighbours.

Practical and financial considerations

- Account for all moving-related expenses, including removal services, packing materials, and any professional cleaning needed for your old or new home.

- Set aside a small contingency fund for unexpected expenses that may arise during the move.

- Make sure your home insurance covers your new property from the day you move in. Some insurance policies also cover items during the move, so check with your provider.

24. DO I NEED STORAGE?

Whether or not you need storage, or a self storage unit, really depends on how many things you have, vs how much space you have to put those things whilst you go through the process of moving.

Home Buyer's Essentials

You might not be familiar with self storage but it's actually quite straight forward – it is not as complex as renting a house; think more like renting a car. It helps if you remember that renting a storage unit is just another temporary tool to make your life easier.

[Full disclosure at this point, I founded SelfStorageBooker.com because I couldn't believe there wasn't already an easy online site where you could just see what storage space was available, at what price, and book it...... fortunately, that site now exists!]

Many people find having somewhere to store all or some of their things liberating when moving house as it can allow them to;

- Declutter their home and make it more appealing to prospective buyers, whilst not having to part with things permanently.

- Carry out renovations/spruce up before selling their house.

- Have more time and space to redecorate their new home and carry out essential bits of maintenance/improvements with less clutter.

- Pack away most of their things leaving only the essentials to move on moving day, making moving costs potentially cheaper and the day less stressful.

- Sell their current house even if their new home isn't ready yet.

- Sell their house and live in rental accommodation whilst they continue searching for their perfect home, at which point they are not in a full chain and are ready to move quickly.

- Move into their new home without having to instantly decide where everything is going to go. Instead, they can carefully select from storage the items they think will work where, and then decide which items they no longer need.

- Have more time if they're downsizing but haven't had chance to part with the things they don't have space for.

- If they have items of furniture they want to sell, depending on the individual storage facility's access policy, they could meet the buyers at the storage unit rather than inviting them to their home.

- Potentially collect in the storage unit new items of furniture and essentials in the run up to getting the keys – especially if they are buying a house for the first time.

Cost considerations

Costs vary depending on where in the country you are and the type of storage you choose. For an illustrated guide to the different types visit https://selfstoragebooker.com/blog/the-different-types-of-self-storage-a-guide-to-finding-the-perfect-fit.

As of 2025 including VAT:

- A typical **160 square foot storage container**, which is handy for a 3-bedroom house move, could be from £30 a week, (£130 per month), in parts of Yorkshire, to £100 a week, (£435 per month), in parts of London.

- A typical **75 square foot indoor storage room**, which is handy for a 2-bedroom apartment move, could be from £35 a week, (£152 per month), in parts of Tyne and Wear, to £47 a week, (£204 per month), in parts of Oxford.

Practical considerations

- Self storage is often rented in quantities of square feet.

Home Buyer's Essentials

- Think about what things you would like to put into storage and approximately how much space you might need. For example, an average single garage is approximately 100 square feet.

- You can find self storage options online and check out customer reviews, before deciding on the best storage facility/unit for you.

- Most customers decide which storage facility to use based on a combination of convenience, price, security and amenities - relevant to their needs.

- Before moving into your self storage unit you will likely be asked:

  - What date/time you would like to move in

  - Whether you have an idea of how long you would like to store for, (but don't worry storage is usually a rolling contract so you don't have to know for sure)

  - Whether you have insurance or whether you would like to add this on to the rent – approx. value of your goods to support this.

  - ID check

  - Refundable deposit

  - Sign a Storage Agreement

- When you move into your storage unit make the most of all of the space i.e. stack the things that are safe to and put the things you will need last to the back of the unit.

25. WHY IS IT GOOD TO BE A "GOOD BUYER"?

Being a good buyer is helpful because it means you might be favoured by the house seller. If you are in a competitive market this could mean your offer is more likely to be accepted than another buyer. It may also mean that the seller has more faith that you will successfully complete on the purchase, and so if they are keen to move quickly, they may be more open to negotiating on price.

To someone selling their home, or an estate agent acting for them, a "good buyer" is typically seen as someone who can make the transaction as smooth, swift and stress-free as possible.

Key characteristics;

Financial readiness

- A buyer who already has a mortgage agreement in principle, has proof of funds or is a cash buyer is very attractive. It indicates that the buyer is serious and financially capable of completing the purchase.

- A buyer who has a substantial deposit ready (typically 10-25% of the purchase price) is seen as less risky and more likely to secure mortgage approval.

- A buyer who has a good and reliable income and is likely to be favoured by financial lenders.

No chain or short chain (see Tip 26)

- A buyer who does not need to sell another property to buy the seller's home is highly desirable. This reduces the chances of delays or the deal falling through because of problems elsewhere in the chain.

- If the buyer is in a chain, a shorter chain is preferable, as it minimises the risk of complications and delays.

Quick decision-making

- A buyer who makes a prompt and reasonable offer is seen positively. Sellers prefer buyers who are decisive and do not drag out the negotiation process.

- A buyer who responds quickly to queries and requests, such as providing necessary documents or scheduling surveys, is viewed as cooperative and serious about the purchase.

Flexibility and cooperation

- A buyer who is flexible on the completion date or willing to compromise on minor issues (e.g., leaving fixtures and fittings) is seen as easier to work with.

- A buyer who negotiates respectfully, without making unrealistic demands, fosters a positive relationship and builds trust with the seller.

Professional representation

- A buyer who has engaged a reputable solicitor or conveyancer is appealing because it indicates the legal process will be handled efficiently and professionally.

- If the buyer is using a mortgage broker, it suggests that they are serious about securing financing and have expert support to navigate the mortgage process.

Genuine interest

- A buyer who shows genuine interest in the property and is enthusiastic about making it their home can be more attractive to sellers, particularly if the seller has an emotional attachment to the property.

Commitment and reliability

- A buyer who is committed to the purchase and demonstrates reliability by keeping to agreed timelines and fulfilling their obligations is positively regarded.

- Buyers who are ready to move quickly, especially those who have already completed other due diligence like surveys and legal checks, are viewed as more serious and desirable.

26. WHAT IS A CHAIN?

One of the most delicate aspects of buying or selling a home here in the UK is navigating the property chain. Too often "the chain collapsed" is cited by emotionally and financially injured buyers and sellers throughout the chain as they explain their disappointment at not being able to move.

A chain refers to the sequence of linked property transactions where each purchase relies on the successful completion of another. These chains can range from simple, involving just two parties, to highly complex, with multiple buyers and sellers depending on each other.

Understanding how property chains work, and what happens when they go right—or wrong—is helpful to manage expectations.

When a chain forms

- Each buyer and seller relies on the successful completion of another sale.

- Often a first-time or cash buyer who doesn't need to sell a property starts the chain.

- Someone who isn't purchasing another property, such as someone moving into rented accommodation or downsizing usually ends the chain.

Example of a chain

- ∞ Buyer A wants to purchase Owner B's house....

- ∞ In order for Owner B to sell to Buyer A, they need to buy another house to move into, from Owner C; but Owner B needs the money from their sale to Buyer A to pay Owner C.....

- ∞ In order for Owner C to sell to Owner B, they need to buy another house to move into, from Owner D; but Owner C needs the money from their sale to Owner B to pay Owner D.....

and so on....

When chains go right

- Smooth financing and surveys: Mortgage approvals and property surveys are completed without delays or major issues.

- Clear communication: Estate agents, solicitors, and buyers/sellers communicate regularly, resolving any concerns promptly.

- Contract exchanges: All parties agree and exchange contracts, legally committing to the transactions.

- Realistic completion dates: Everyone in the chain has sufficient time to pack, move, and complete their transactions.

- Outcome: When everything goes right, (rarely entirely stress free), all parties complete their transactions on the agreed dates, and everyone moves into their new homes seamlessly.

When chains go wrong (also see example delays in Tip 2)

- Buyers or sellers pulling out: If one party withdraws, the chain may collapse entirely.

- Financing issues: Delays or denials in mortgage approval, or proof of source of funds can hold up transactions.

- Survey problems: Serious issues uncovered during surveys, such as structural damage, may cause buyers to reconsider their purchase or try to renegotiate the purchase price.

- Unrealistic completion dates: Tight timelines can cause stress and logistical challenges for buyers and sellers.

- Gazumping: A seller accepts a higher offer from a different buyer after initially agreeing to a sale.

- Gazundering: A buyer lowers their offer at the last minute.

How to reduce the risks in a chain

- Opt for chain-free or simple chain purchases.

- A reliable solicitor or conveyancer ensures smooth handling of legal work and quick resolution of issues.

- Stay in touch with all parties, including estate agents and solicitors, routinely and keep a record of dates and actions, to address concerns early.

- Obtain a mortgage agreement in principle before starting your property search to prevent delays.

- Break the chain by selling your own and renting a house temporarily, or using self storage to provide flexibility if your chain is delayed (see Tip 24).

FINANCIALS

27. HOW MUCH DOES THE PROCESS COST?

When buying a house, the actual cost goes beyond the purchase price, (which you have hopefully negotiated well on!). You'll need to consider various additional costs, including stamp duty, legal fees, survey costs, and mortgage-related expenses. These will vary depending on the property size and value.

Key cost considerations

Stamp Duty Land Tax (SDLT)

- Payable on the purchase of all freeholds and leaseholds, (see Tips 57 and 58), and shared ownership schemes, (see Tips 11 and 21).

England:

- From April 2025: SDLT is paid on residential property purchases over £125,000 and non-residential property/land purchases over £150,000.

- The rates apply as a percentage of the property price. They are calculated by the proportion of the property's value within the bracket of each threshold i.e:

    - 2% paid on £125,001 to £250,000

    - 5% paid on £250,001 to £925,000

    - 10% paid on £925,001 to £1.5 million

    - 12% on the value above £1.5 million

Home Buyer's Essentials

- First time buyers have an increased threshold of £300,000, provided the property is worth £500,000 or less.

- Rates also vary if you are buying this as an additional property or you're not a UK resident.

Wales:

- The Land Transaction Tax (LTT) replaced SDLT in 2018.

- It is payable on the purchase of all residential properties over £225,000 and all non-residential properties/land over £225,000 also.

- Higher rates may apply if you own more than one residential property of are buying as a company.

- There is no first-time buyers' relief in Wales.

- The rates apply as a percentage of the property price. They are calculated by the proportion of the property's value within the bracket of each threshold i.e:

    - 6% paid on £225,001 to £400,000
    - 7.5% paid on £400,001 to £750,000
    - 10% paid on £750,001 to £1.5 million
    - 12% on the value above £1.5 million

Mortgage fees

- Booking fee: Some lenders charge £100 – £200 for this.

- Arrangement/product fee: Typically, between £0 and £2,000, depending on the lender and mortgage product.

- Valuation fee: Can range from £0 to £1,500 based on the property's value and the lender's policies

- Mortgage account fee: Some lenders charge £100 - £300 for this.

- Be clear on what mortgage fees will be charged by your lender. They may bulk them together into one. Fees can often be added to the mortgage itself but be aware that you will likely pay interest on them for the duration of the loan.

- Check if any fees are refundable if the mortgage doesn't go ahead.

- If you are using a mortgage broker, be sure to factor in their fees too if they are extra.

- In addition to upfront costs be clear on longer term lending costs i.e. the interest payable on the mortgage and possible early repayment fees for example.

- Whilst not an additional cost in itself, you will need to factor into your cashflow, the value of the mortgage deposit which will normally be paid at exchange of contracts via the buyer's and seller's solicitors.

Legal fees

- Solicitor/conveyancer fees: Usually between £900 and £3,000 plus VAT.

- Check what their fee includes. There could be additional fees to pay such as "searches" around £200, anti-money laundering checks around £20, CHAPS transfer fee approx. £30 and Land Registry around £300. These all vary depending on the property value, location and complexity.

- Some solicitors may require an upfront initial fee which is usually 10% of their total fee with the remaining paid when the purchase is completed.

Survey costs

- Basic valuation: Often covered or charged by the lender; see mortgage fees. Alternatively, you can instruct an independent registered RICS valuer, (advisable if you are not taking out a mortgage); who can cost between £450 and £1,500.
- Level 2 Home Survey (Home Buyer's Report): Typically costs between £400 and £1,000.
- Level 3 Building Survey (Full Structural Survey): Costs between £600 and £2,000, depending on the property size, location and condition.

Moving costs

- Removal services: Can range from £400 to £3,000+, depending on distance and amount of belongings

Insurance

- Buildings and contents insurance: Costs vary based on property value, location, and coverage level, typically ranging from £100 to £1500 per year. Buildings insurance is mandatory for many mortgage lenders.

Estate agent's fees

- If you are selling a home too, don't forgot to factor in the estate agent's fees, if you are using one. Usually this is 1% - 3% of the final sale price, plus VAT. Some estate agents charge a flat fee.

Home Buyer's Essentials

- Buyers don't usually pay estate agency fees, but some online estate agencies charge a "purchaser fee". It is important to check this and factor it into your budget.

Below are examples of some of the costs associated with buying houses of different values. These are very broad indications (with no context of complexity or location), and don't include provision for First Time Buyer incentives or seller-based fees, (such as estate agent), etc.

Property Value	Stamp Duty	Mortgage Fees inc. Valuation	Legal Fees	Level 2 Survey Costs	Moving Costs	Building Insurance Costs
£125,000	£0	£1,750	£850	£550	£600	£200
£150,000	£500	£1,750	£900	£550	£700	£300
£250,000	£2,500	£1,750	£1,100	£600	£950	£350
£350,000	£7,500	£1,850	£1,500	£650	£1,100	£400
£450,000	£12,500	£1,950	£1,500	£650	£1,250	£500
£550,000	£17,500	£2,050	£1,500	£700	£1,500	£600
£650,000	£22,500	£2,150	£1,500	£750	£1,750	£700
£750,000	£27,500	£2,250	£1,600	£750	£2,000	£800
£850,000	£32,500	£2,350	£1,600	£800	£2,250	£900
£950,000	£38,750	£2,450	£1,700	£950	£2,500	£1,000
£1,050,000	£48,750	£2,550	£1,800	£1,100	£2,750	£1,100

28. AM I GOING TO BE ABLE TO AFFORD IT?

Even when you have calculated the affordability of your mortgage and upfront costs there are other financial considerations. The chances are many of these will already be on your radar, but here are a few tips to bear in mind. Note, costs are based on 2025 industry quoted average examples.

Income and outgoings

- Assess your monthly income, including salary, bonuses, and any additional sources of income. Lenders typically look for stable income over a period of time, typically six months to a year.

- Calculate your debt-to-income (DTI) ratio, which compares your monthly debt payments to your gross monthly income. Lenders prefer a DTI ratio of 39% or less.

- Use an online mortgage calculator to estimate how much you can borrow based on your income and expenses. This tool can help you understand what your monthly mortgage payments would be and how they fit into your budget.

- A general rule is that your monthly mortgage payment should not exceed 28-30% of your gross monthly income. Certainly, the lower this number is the easier it will likely be for you to get a mortgage. Some buyers may choose to pay more to clear their mortgage faster for example and save interest fees in the longer run.

- If this is your first house be sure to factor in running costs, (otherwise known as household bills), which you might not currently incur including, council tax, service charge (if applicable), electric, gas/oil, water/sewerage, phone/internet, house insurance, TV licence.

- There are various "% rules" quoted about how much you should be spending on bills and mortgage costs relative to your income. Generally, it would be wise if costs/debt and mortgage payments don't exceed more than 36% of your income.

- Consider how a potential increase in interest rates would affect your mortgage payments. Lenders often stress-test borrowers by assessing their ability to afford payments at higher rates.

- Consider your job security and any future changes in income that could impact your ability to pay the mortgage and other household bills.

- Account for any future expenses like starting a family, which could increase your outgoings and affect your ability to manage mortgage payments.

- Maintain an emergency fund equivalent to three to six months' worth of expenses to cover unexpected costs like essential repairs or a temporary loss of income.

Ongoing costs

- The interest rate on your mortgage will significantly impact your monthly payments, which is why it's so important to get the best deal you can. At the time of writing a typical 2-year fixed mortgage deal has an interest rate of 5.5%. This means in your first year for an average £200,000 mortgage, with a 25% deposit and a loan term of 25 years, you will be paying £681 in interest alone each month and only £239 a month off the balance of the mortgage. This ratio improves the longer you have your mortgage and the less balance there is remaining.

Home Buyer's Essentials

- Ensure you understand the difference between fixed-rate and variable-rate mortgages and choose what suits your financial situation (see Tip 30).

- Building and contents insurance costs vary based on property value, location, and coverage level, typically ranging from £100 to £1500 per year. Buildings insurance is mandatory for a lot of mortgage lenders.

- Gas, electricity, water, and internet costs typically amount to £2,000 to £3,500+ per year, depending on usage and location.

- Council tax rates vary by local authority and the property's valuation band. Higher-value properties typically fall into higher bands, resulting in higher council tax. In 2024 council tax could be anywhere between £1,100 and £5,087 per year. The average being just over £2,000 a year.

- Example monthly household bills including mortgage:

Cost	1-bed house	2-bed house	3-bed house	4-bed house
Mortgage	£800	£1,300	£1,450	£1,700
Council tax	£150	£213	£252	£291
Electricity	£60	£81	£96	£112
Gas/oil	£53	£76	£91	£107
Water/sewerage	£34	£37	£42	£46
Internet	£29	£29	£29	£29
TV Licence	£13	£13	£13	£13
Total per month	**£1,139**	**£1,749**	**£1,973**	**£2,298**

Important note: these figures are industry approximate averages and will vary based on individual circumstances, service providers, location, house size/value and usage patterns.

- If you regularly attend to routine maintenance of your home, you can avoid more significant issues which could cost you more. For example, a simple leaking/blocked gutter could, over time, concentrate water on roof timbers which can decay and lead to having to replace part of the roof structure! As a minimum, budget for routinely clearing out gutters and gullies, servicing heating systems, replacing missing slates etc (see Tip 37).

- Set aside a savings fund for bigger repairs/replacement which will arise throughout the life the building. The typical life expectancy of some more common items include;

    - uPVC windows and doors – 25 years
    - Gas boilers – 15 years
    - Render or claddings – 30 years
    - Flat roof covering – 25 years
    - Various pitched roof coverings – 50 – 100 years

29. WHAT ARE THE BIG COST RISKS?

Despite best endeavours there will be times when buying or owning a house that you're struck with an unforeseen cost. It is helpful to at least be aware of where and when these could arise, so that you can manage how much you commit beforehand. Here are some of the more common examples.

Repair and renovation costs

Risk. Properties may require more repairs or renovations than initially apparent. Issues like water ingress and structural movement can lead to substantial costs that were not anticipated during the initial purchase. However more often a simple lack of maintenance or modernisation from the previous owners can leave you with a hefty financial burden in the forthcoming years.

Mitigation. Conduct thorough surveys before purchase (see Tip 3 for help choosing the relevant survey type). Items to look out for on the survey report that could potentially be more costly, include;

- Rebuilding chimney stacks
- Re-roofing
- Larger scale leadwork replacement
- Addressing structural movement or defects, including foundation issues
- Re-rendering
- Replacing windows and doors, especially if installing more specialist units such as timber framed sash windows, (the type that slide vertically)
- Replacing floor structures
- Addressing dry rot (see Tip 37)
- Asbestos removal
- Issues with cavity wall ties
- Issues with cavity or external wall insulation
- Re-wiring
- New heating or plumbing systems
- New below ground drainage systems
- Re-building larger retaining walls
- Rebuilding stone walls
- Re-surfacing driveways

- Removing large trees
- Dealing with invasive species such as Japanese Knotweed
- Dealing with unauthorised statutory consent issues, such as alterations to a listed building without official approval (see Tip 61)

Rising interest rates

Risk. If you have a variable-rate mortgage or your fixed rate is set to expire, an increase in interest rates can significantly raise your monthly mortgage payments, affecting your affordability.

Mitigation. Speak to your lender or seek advice from a professional Mortgage Broker and consider locking in a fixed-rate mortgage for a longer term to protect against future rate rises. Ensure you budget for potential increases when your fixed rate ends.

Stamp Duty Land Tax (SDLT) miscalculations

Risk. Misunderstanding or underestimating the amount of Stamp Duty you will need to pay, (or Land Transaction Tax in Wales), can lead to unexpected financial strain. The tax scales with the property price and has different rates for first-time buyers, second homes, and investment properties.

Mitigation. Use reliable Stamp Duty calculators to get an accurate estimate, and confirm these with your solicitor, (and run by your accountant if you have one), before committing to a purchase. Be aware of any reliefs or exemptions you might qualify for.

Legal and conveyancing fees

Risk. Legal fees can increase due to complications such as issues with the title deeds, disputes over boundaries, or problems discovered during searches. These costs can escalate if additional legal work is required.

Mitigation. Obtain a detailed quote from your solicitor before proceeding and ask about potential additional costs. Ensure you are clear on what is and isn't included in the scope of their instruction. Be thorough in conducting and understanding all necessary searches and investigations, so that problems can be identified early before incurring more expense.

Property value fluctuations

Risk. Market conditions can cause the value of your property to fall, especially if you buy at the peak of the market. This can lead to negative equity if property prices drop, which is particularly concerning if you need to sell the property soon after purchase. The value of your house could also be affected if something changes in the local area, such as an unwelcome property development on adjoining land or property taxation changes.

Mitigation. Research the local property market and buy with a long-term view. Avoid overextending yourself financially and be cautious of market trends. Take professional advice to ensure that the price you are paying is a fair value for the property. Ensure that local searches identify any potential planning applications, permissions or land re-designations which could affect the value of your house in future. Keep an eye on local press which could feature news that might affect your property.

30. HOW DO I GET A MORTGAGE?

For many people being able to obtain a mortgage is mission critical when it comes to buying a house. It typically involves several steps, from assessing your financial situation to securing the best deal, but the earlier you can start planning for it the better. For example, if you know that home ownership is for you and you will need a mortgage, you can start saving for a deposit or aligning your career/business and life plans so that when the time comes you are in the best position you can be.

Assess your financial situation

- Check your credit score through agencies like Experian, Equifax or Clear Score. A higher credit score can improve your chances of getting a mortgage and securing a better interest rate.

- Evaluate your income, expenses, and any existing debts. Lenders will assess your affordability based on these factors. Ideally the percentage of your monthly income that goes towards paying your debts, including the new mortgage you will be paying, i.e. your debt-to-income (DTI) ratio, should be below 39%.

- If you are self-employed or own your own company demonstrating your income can be more involved and will usually require providing copies of the last several years of your year-end tax self-assessments or company accounts.

- Secure a deposit. Whether this is through savings, sale of an asset, inheritance/gift or winning the lottery; generally, you need at least 5% to 20% of the property's value. A larger deposit can give you access to better mortgage deals and potentially more leniency in terms of the property condition/surveys. You will need to provide proof of where the deposit came from to comply with anti-money laundering laws. Some mortgage lenders won't accept deposits from crypto currency.

- Be aware that the lender may also review your spending habits and will not look favourably on activity such as spending lots of money on online gambling or taking out payday loans. If you know you will be applying for a mortgage in the future it is time to start making your spending habits look sensible.

Research mortgage options

- The reason you are buying the house will determine the type of mortgage you require. e.g. if you are buying it to rent it out a conventional owner occupier mortgage won't do.

- The main mortgage types to decide between are a fixed-rate mortgage (interest rate stays the same for a set period) or a variable-rate mortgage or tracker mortgage (interest rate can change). Fixed-rate mortgages offer stability, while variable rates may offer lower initial interest rates but can fluctuate.

- Other mortgage options include Joint Borrower Sole Proprietor mortgages (JBSP), a Guarantor Mortgage (also known as a family-assisted mortgage), and an Offset Mortgage.

- Consider the length of the mortgage term, typically 25 years, but it can be longer or shorter. A shorter term means higher monthly payments, but less interest paid overall.

- If you're a first-time buyer, consider government schemes like First Homes or Shared Ownership to help you get on the property ladder (see Tip 11).

- Use online mortgage calculators to estimate how much you can borrow and what your monthly repayments will be. This will help you understand what you can afford and narrow down your property search.

- Obtain an initial mortgage illustration to gauge what you could be able to lend. This can help both you and prospective sellers/estate agents understand whether you are searching for houses of a realistic value.

- Don't forget to factor in other upfront and ongoing costs such as Stamp Duty, legal fees, survey fees, and home insurance (see Tip 27).

- Check whether your preferred lender has any specific criteria which will make it difficult for them to grant the mortgage you need. There could be various reasons, and not all lenders are the same. For example, some lenders won't grant a mortgage for properties;
    - of "non-standard construction"
    - with fewer than a certain number of years on a leasehold
    - properties in certain locations/positions
    - certain structural issues or building features
    - properties with certain restrictions e.g. an agricultural tie
    - houses accompanied with more than a certain number of acres

Obtain a Mortgage Agreement in Principle (AIP)

- Get a Mortgage Agreement in Principle from a lender. This shows sellers that you are serious and have the financial backing to proceed. It's not a guarantee of a mortgage but gives you an idea of what you might be able to borrow.

- You can get an AIP from multiple lenders without commitment, which can help you compare potential offers. Be aware however that multiple credit checks on your file in a short window can suggest you are a risky borrower.

- The lender will carry out ID and credit checks, review evidence of a deposit and check your income.

- Be aware a Mortgage Agreement in Principle usually expires in 30-90 days from the issue date.

Consider using a Mortgage Broker

- Speaking to a mortgage broker about your plans for the future can help you decide on the best mortgage features, navigate the mortgage market, find the best deals, and handle the application process. Brokers may be able to access deals that aren't available directly to consumers.

- Some brokers are independent and can search the whole market, while others are tied to specific lenders. Ensure you understand the broker's range and fees before proceeding.

- Check that your chosen mortgage broker is regulated by the Financial Conduct Authority (FCA).

Apply for the mortgage

- Be prepared to provide extensive documentation, including proof of income (e.g., several months payslips, tax returns), bank statements, ID, and details of any existing debts.

- Once you've chosen a lender, they will conduct a full assessment of your application. This includes a hard credit check and usually a property valuation.

- If approved, the lender will issue a formal mortgage offer, which you can then use to proceed with your property purchase.

Complete the purchase

- Once you have your mortgage offer, speak with your solicitor who will handle the legal process, including property searches, contract signing, and transferring funds (see Tip 2).

- Before completion, ensure that all mortgage terms are clear, and you understand your obligations as a borrower.

- Ensure you have complied with any specific terms the lender may have, for example if they require you to hold certain insurances.

Manage your mortgage

- Ensure you set up your mortgage payments and keep up with them to avoid penalties or even repossession of your home.

- Periodically review your mortgage, especially as your fixed rate comes to an end. You may be able to switch to a better deal.

- Ensure you are complying with the mortgage terms; for example, you may be required to notify your lender if you change jobs or decide to holiday let your home.

31. WHAT HAPPENS TO MY DEPOSIT?

Firstly, congratulations on forming a deposit for a house – an achievement in itself. It is a lot of money and it's natural that you would like to know what happens to it when it leaves your hands.

Holding deposit (before exchange of contracts)

- You may be asked to pay a holding deposit to reserve the property while the legal processes are being completed. This is usually payable via the estate agent.

- The amount can vary, and it is important to ensure the deposit is part payment of the purchase price and not an additional charge.

- You must get a written agreement for the deposit which includes the conditions upon which it may be returned/or not, e.g. if you decide not to go ahead with the purchase, you may lose this deposit.

Exchange of contracts

- At the exchange of contracts, you usually pay a deposit of 10% of the property's purchase price via your solicitor. This is a significant step where the sale becomes legally binding. Both you and the seller are committed to completing the transaction.

- The deposit is held by the seller's solicitor or conveyancer in a client account until the completion date. It's not accessible to the seller during this period, ensuring that the funds are secure.

Completion

- On completion day, via your solicitor, the full purchase price of the property (minus the deposit already paid) is transferred from your mortgage lender and your funds (if applicable) to the seller's solicitor. Their solicitor then transfers the deposit, along with the remaining balance, to the seller.

- Once the seller's solicitor confirms receipt of the full funds, the ownership of the property is officially transferred to you, and you can collect the keys.

Risks and forfeiture

- If you, as the buyer, fail to complete the purchase after exchanging contracts, you risk losing your deposit. This is a legal measure to compensate the seller for the failed transaction.

- If the seller fails to complete after exchange of contracts, you are entitled to get your deposit back, and you could potentially claim compensation for additional costs incurred due to the failed purchase.

Deposit protection (for new-builds)

- If you're buying a new-build property, your deposit might be protected by a scheme such as the National House Building Council (NHBC) or a similar insurance-backed guarantee. This ensures that your deposit is safe if the builder fails to complete the property.

32. HOW DO I KNOW IF I'M BUYING THE HOUSE FOR THE RIGHT PRICE?

Determining whether you're buying a house for the right price can be rather frustrating. If you require, a mortgage the lender's valuation surveyor will make an assessment, which will be shared with you and the lender. This is to ensure the value of the property would cover the amount being lent in the worst case that the house has to be repossessed and sold.

If you are not lending money to buy the house, you may wish to appoint an RICS Chartered Valuation Surveyor to provide an independent valuation and gain confidence that your investment is wise.

There are also other steps that you can take to gauge whether you are paying a fair price:

Research comparable properties

- Look at the sold prices of similar properties in the same area (known as comparables or "comps"). These properties should be similar in size, condition, age, and location and you will need to consider price changes over time. This will give you a benchmark for what homes in the area are selling for. Websites like Zoopla, Rightmove and the Land Registry are easy sources of information.

- Speak to local estate agents who have a good understanding of the local market. They can provide insights into whether the asking price is in line with current market trends.

Evaluate market conditions

- Understand whether you're in a buyer's or seller's market. In a seller's market, demand outstrips supply, often driving prices higher. In a buyer's market, there's more supply than demand, which can lead to lower prices. This context can help you understand if the price is inflated and whether it's a good time to buy.

- Look at the overall property market trends. Are prices in the area rising, stable, or falling? Websites like the Office for National Statistics (ONS) provide data on house price trends across the UK in the form of "House price data: quarterly tables".

Assess property condition

- Obtain a professional survey from an RICS Chartered Building Surveyor. These reports can reveal potential issues like water ingress, structural problems, or the need for expensive repairs. If significant issues are found, you may decide to negotiate a lower price to offset how much you will potentially spend to address them. Of course, this doesn't necessarily mean that the seller will entertain negotiations, especially if the property/area is in demand or they feel the price is reflective of its condition.

- Consider any renovation or repair costs you'll need to undertake after purchase. Add these costs to the purchase price to evaluate whether the total investment makes sense and is affordable.

Consider long-term value

- Evaluate the long-term potential of the property. Is the area up-and-coming, with plans for new transport links, schools, or amenities? These factors can add to the property's value over time.

- Think about how easy it will be to sell the property in the future. Factors like location, school catchment areas, quality of local healthcare and proximity to transport links play a significant role in resale value.

Negotiate

- If your research suggests the property is overpriced, don't be afraid to make an offer below the asking price. Use the information from comparables, valuations, and any identified issues to justify your offer, and explain this rationale to the vendors/estate agents.

- Understand the seller's situation. A seller who wants to move quickly or who has had the property on the open market for a long time may be more willing to accept a lower offer.

33. WHAT SHOULD I KNOW ABOUT SERVICE CHARGES?

Service charges are payments made by leaseholders (or possibly freeholders in some developments) to the freeholder, landlord, or managing agent of a property. These charges cover the costs of maintaining and managing the communal areas of a building or estate. Service charges are most commonly associated with flats but can also apply to houses in certain developments, particularly in private estates (see Tip 13). (To note, there are some significant legislation changes in the pipeline in respect of leaseholds, with "commonholds" set to replace them; refer to glossary and take further advice in this respect).

Service charges can vary depending on the property and the agreement but generally cover:

- Maintenance, such as cleaning communal areas, gardening, and general repairs (e.g., fixing a leaky roof or replacing worn-out carpets in common areas).

- Buildings insurance for the entire block, covering structural damage to the property (this typically doesn't cover contents).

- Shared utility costs, such as electricity for lighting communal areas, water for gardens, or heating in shared spaces.

- Fees paid to managing agents who oversee the day-to-day management of the property.

- Reserve or sinking fund; contributions towards a fund that is set aside for major works or unexpected large expenses, such as replacing a roof or major structural repairs.

- Costs associated with security services, such as CCTV, security staff, or entry systems.

Service charges are usually calculated based on the size of the property or its proportionate share of the total costs. The details should be outlined in the lease, or the transfer document for freeholders. The landlord or managing agent will estimate the annual cost and then apportion this among the leaseholders. Sometimes, service charges are fixed, but they are often variable, meaning they can increase or decrease based on actual costs incurred.

Things to expect

- Leaseholders have the right to challenge unreasonable service charges through the First-tier Tribunal (Property Chamber) in England or the Leasehold Valuation Tribunal in Wales.

- Leaseholders are entitled to a breakdown of service charges and have the right to inspect accounts, receipts, and other documents relating to the service charges.

- If the landlord intends to carry out major works costing more than £250 per leaseholder, they are legally required to consult with the leaseholders. Failure to do so can limit the amount the landlord can recover. This is typically called a "Section 20" notice, (in reference to the Landlord and Tenant Act 1985).

- Separate from service charges, some leaseholders are required to pay ground rent i.e. for the right to occupy the land the building sits on. Ground rent for new leases has been abolished in England and Wales.

Things to be aware of

- Service charges can increase significantly over time, especially if major repairs or renovations are needed. These costs can sometimes become unaffordable.

- Some leaseholders find it difficult to obtain detailed breakdowns or understand how their money is being spent, leading to disputes or dissatisfaction.

- In the absence of a sufficient reserve fund, leaseholders can be charged large one-off bills for unexpected major works, like a new roof or elevator repairs.

- Disagreements over service charges can lead to legal disputes, which can be time-consuming and costly for all parties involved.

- High or increasing service charges can make a property less attractive to potential buyers, potentially reducing its market value.

Mitigating the risks

- Understand the terms of your lease regarding service charges, including how they are calculated and what they cover.

- Note how well maintained the property is and if it looks like major repairs or modernisations are likely to arise. A Chartered Surveyor can carry out a survey to support this (see Tip 3).

- Take professional advice before committing to buy the property, and at any time you're unsure about service charges during your ownership.

- Ensure you receive regular, detailed statements showing how service charges are spent. This helps ensure transparency and can alert you to potential issues.

- Read tenant communications and attend tenant meetings if held.

- If possible, get involved with the Tenants Association (TA)/Residents' Association if there is one. Depending on the circumstances leaseholders could also take over management through the Right to Manage process.

- Always budget for potential increases in service charges, especially if you know major works are planned or if the reserve fund is low or there isn't one in place.

34. WHAT DOES "NEGATIVE EQUITY" MEAN?

Negative equity occurs when the value of a property falls below the outstanding balance on the mortgage secured against it.

This situation is most common when property prices decline after purchasing a property, particularly if it was bought with a small deposit or a large percentage of the property's value was lent against.

Example 1: A small drop in house value

- You buy a house for £200,000 with a 10% deposit of £20,000 and a mortgage of £180,000.

- A few years later, due to a downturn in the property market, the value of your home falls to £170,000.

- Your outstanding mortgage is still around £175,000 (assuming you've made some repayments).

- This means your property is now worth less than your mortgage debt—by £5,000. This is negative equity.

Example 2: A significant market downturn

- You buy a house for £300,000 with a 5% deposit (£15,000) and a mortgage of £285,000.

- The property market crashes, and your home's value drops to £250,000.

- If your mortgage balance is still around £280,000, you are now £30,000 in negative equity, as the house is worth much less than the amount owed on the mortgage.

Why negative equity matters

- If you need to sell your home while in negative equity, the sale proceeds won't cover the remaining mortgage balance. You would need to make up the difference from your own funds or wait until market conditions potentially improve.

- Negative equity makes it difficult to remortgage or switch to a better mortgage deal, as lenders typically require some equity in the property to offer competitive rates.

- Negative equity tends to become more common during economic downturns when property prices are falling and unemployment is rising, which can lead to increased financial stress for homeowners.

Managing negative equity

- By putting down a larger deposit when purchasing a home, you reduce the risk of falling into negative equity if property prices decline.

- Making regular overpayments on your mortgage can help reduce the outstanding balance faster, thereby reducing the risk of negative equity.

- If you find yourself in negative equity, it's often best to stay in the property and continue paying down the mortgage. Over time, property values may recover, and your mortgage balance will decrease, eventually bringing you out of negative equity.

35. WHAT IF I'M BUYING THE HOUSE PURELY AS AN INVESTMENT?

Firstly, if this is solely a financial investment, then you are strongly advised to take professional financial advice. The Financial Conduct Authority (FCA) has a register of authorised firms to give you greater protection.

There are plenty who boast that investing in houses is a great idea, however there are many financial experts who would advise there are more compelling investments, or blend of investments, you could make, which would likely yield more satisfactory results. Indeed, an evaluation of this very topic would make a substantial book in itself.

At the very least if you're buying a house purely as an investment, you would be wise to consider it in the context of your wider investment strategy and take professional advice accordingly.

There is often a misconception that property, once invested in, is a relatively passive asset. However, it takes careful planning and decision making, as well as a degree of good fortune, to ensure maintenance liabilities, taxation and building occupant headaches do not chip in to your bottom line.

Home Buyer's Essentials

Below, are just some of the aspects to consider which could help to make your house investment sounder and more profitable.

Location

- Location is crucial in real estate investment. Choose areas with high demand for rental properties or strong potential for property value appreciation. Consider proximity to amenities, good schools, transport links, and employment hubs.

- High rental demand in the area ensures a steady stream of tenants, reducing the risk of vacancy periods.

- Research local market trends. Is the area undergoing regeneration? Are property values and rental prices rising? An area on an upward trend can offer better returns.

- Are there potential risks which could de-value your investment post purchase such as "not in my back yard" (NIMBY) type developments? Or do these offer you the opportunity to buy the property at a lower price?

Type of property

- Consider who your target market is for the location and consider what type of property will attract them. For example, student areas may benefit from HMOs (Houses in Multiple Occupation), while young professionals might prefer modern apartments.

- New builds vs. older properties; new builds may have fewer maintenance issues initially, but older properties might offer better value for money and potential for value-added improvements.

- Freehold vs. leasehold properties (see Tips 57 and 58).

- Renovation project vs. good condition; a renovation project could offer you more scope to add value should your intention be to sell the property quickly, (flip), particularly if you have easy access to skills/labour for example. If you plan to rent the property out, the longer it is uninhabited the less rental income you are making, and this needs to be factored into your costs.

Finance and costs

- Buying the house at the right price is critical, particularly if this is a shorter-term investment e.g. a flip, (buy-add value-sell). It is in the purchase price where you could ultimately make the most return/loss when you eventually sell/rent out.

- Factor in the cost of financing, e.g. buy-to-let mortgages typically require a higher deposit (around 25-40%) and have higher interest rates than residential mortgages. Ensure you have a clear understanding of your financing options, and the costs involved.

- Consider ongoing costs such as property management fees, maintenance, insurance, and void periods where the property might be empty.

Tax implications

- Be aware of higher Stamp Duty or Land Transaction Tax for second homes or buy-to-let properties. Factor this into your budget.

- Income Tax; applicable if you own the property as a personal landlord, rather than a limited company. Rental income, after certain expenses, is subject to Income Tax which could end up being as high as 45% if you earn over the Additional Rate Tax threshold. Alternatively, if you own the property as a company, you will pay Corporation Tax and would also occur tax on dividends i.e. the money taken out of the company for its shareholders.

- Capital Gains Tax (CGT); if you sell the property at a profit, CGT may be payable on the gains up to a rate of 24%.

- Inheritance Tax is charged to beneficiaries of your estate at a rate of 40%, for assets over £325,000. For efficiency, you can instead gift the asset to them while you are alive, provided you live for at least 7 years after, however they may be subject to Capital Gains Tax for the benefit.

- Be aware of recent changes to reliefs for furnished holiday lets. This has affected the profitability of some buy-to-let investments.

- Take professional tax advice to understand the most efficient way for you to invest and release value when you need to. The ownership structure is important and can be one of the key factors in determining whether an investment is financially feasible.

Yield and return on investment (ROI)

- Rental yield can be expressed as gross rental yield and net rental yield; gross rental yield measures your rental income against the value of the property before expenses. Net rental yield is what you'll be left with after expenses.

- Calculate the rental yield, which is the annual rental income divided by the property's value, multiplied by 100 and expressed as a percentage. A good net rental yield typically ranges from 5% to 7%.

- Consider the potential for the property's value to vary over time. Research the historical property price trends in the area.

Home Buyer's Essentials

Legal considerations

- Understand your legal responsibilities as a landlord, including ensuring the property meets safety standards, managing deposits, and maintaining the property.

- Ensure you have a solid tenancy agreement in place that covers all the legal aspects of renting, including notice periods, rent payment terms, and tenant responsibilities. There are a lot of legislative changes happening in this matter. Make sure you know how they will affect you in the long term.

- Take professional legal advice to ensure that you and your asset are protected and aligned with your longer-term investment strategy.

- Legal compliance includes

Tenancy agreement (England) / Standard Occupation Contract (Wales)
Deposit protection in a government approved scheme
Gas safety certificate
Electrical safety certificate
Smoke alarms
Carbon monoxide alarms
Fire safety compliance
Legionella risk assessment
Right to Rent checks (England)
Provide 'How to Rent' guide (England) / written statement of terms (Wales)

Keep the property in good repair and make sure it is safe relative to the Housing Health and Safety Rating System (HHSRS)
HMO License (if applicable)
Selective licensing (England -only applicable in certain areas)
Rent Smart Wales registration (Wales only)
Energy Performance Certificate (EPC)
Furniture fire safety compliance
Rental income declaration to HMRC for taxation
Data protection (GDPR) compliance

Exit strategy

- As with any investment, it is worth considering your long-term plan so that you can more easily align yourself with the desired outcome early on.

- Will you sell the property after a certain period, or is this a long-term investment? Be mindful of market condition changes and potential capital gains tax when selling. Modelling out a viable contingency plan is sensible.

- You might choose to refinance the property after a few years to release equity or secure better mortgage terms. Again, take professional advice and plan for how and when you'll do this.

UNDERSTANDING THE SURVEY REPORTS

36. WHAT ARE THE PARTS OF THE HOUSE CALLED?

Having a basic understanding of the different parts of a house can help you communicate more effectively with contractors, estate agents, and maintenance professionals. It can also help you to understand survey reports more easily.

The RICS helpfully produces a "Typical house diagram", which can be found in an example RICS survey report (see Tip 3).

To elaborate on some of the less commonly known parts:

- Valley: The junction where two roof pitches meet.

- Ridge: The horizontal top line where two roof pitches meet, usually covered with ridge tiles.

- Roofing felt/membrane: The sheet of material/fabric lining underneath roof coverings.

- Hipped roof: More than two roof pitches leaning in together, i.e. the shorter side of the house also has a roof pitch that leans in towards the ridge.

- Hip tile: Tiles which cover the junction of roof pitches in a hipped roof.

- Flashing: The material which dresses over/under the joints of two other coverings, e.g. lead sheet at the junction between roof covering and a wall.

- Eaves: The edge of the roof where it extends beyond the wall of the building.

- Rafters: Lengths of timber which form the roof structure and support the roof pitch from eaves to ridge.

- Purlins: Lengths of timber which form the roof structure and support the rafters horizontally.

- Roof truss: Structural roof frame usually comprising of diagonal, horizontal and vertical timber or metal.

- Roof verge: The edge of roof pitch above the gable.

- Gable end: Wall that forms a triangulated profile to the end of a building with pitched roof verge above.

- Parapet: Continuation of the wall above the line of the roof covering.

- Soffit: The horizontal underside of a part of your house, commonly referred to for the underside of the roof overhang, (eaves).

- Fascia: A vertically mounted board that runs along the edge of the roof sometimes closing the eaves/soffit area. Often supports gutter brackets.

- Barge board: Boards which follow the line of the gable, closing off the edge of roof structure. Usually timber or plastic.

- Cladding: An outer wall covering that protects the house from weather and can add to its appearance. Materials could include timber, brick, plastic, stone, tile or slate.

- SVP, (soil and vent pipe): Vertical pipe which connects to foul drainage and allows the drainage system to vent/pressure balance.

- DPC, (damp proof course): a thin barrier, (usually some form of plastic sheet), which is bedded into walls and intercepts moisture travel.

- Foundations/footings: The base of the house, often made of concrete, which supports the building's structure and distributes its weight to the ground.

37. WHICH PARTS WILL COST ME THE MOST MONEY?

There are some parts of the house which if defective could cost you more money than others.

When researching this book, one respondent commented that they wanted to know which parts of the building/home survey report (see Tip 3), they needed to be concerned about – as in which sections would likely hurt their pocket the most.

It is important to point out however, that often some of the most expensive repairs could have been avoided by paying attention to simple building maintenance early on, for example fixing a roof slate when it first came loose or clearing gutters. Therefore, it is worth heeding the recommendations throughout the professional reports to save yourself time, money and potential stress in the long run.

Roof and chimney

Re-roofing work, (that is replacing the watertight layer over your house), or rebuilding a chimney stack can be costly. Not only are there the costs involved with undertaking the largely disruptive and potentially hazardous work itself, there is likely to also be substantial access costs for e.g. scaffolding.

Typically, re-roofing, (assuming you can keep the existing roof timbers), could cost anything between £3,000 - £20,000, however a large country residence for example could easily escalate to £100,000.

Re-building a single chimney stack could cost anywhere from £1,000 - £5,000, but again depending on the size, complexity, type of property and location, costs could be well in excess of this.

Foundations

Issues with foundations, such as subsidence, are often identified by observing symptoms of building movement that demonstrate an incapacity for the foundations or surrounding ground to carry the weight of the building above.

The foundations of the house are more than likely underground. Naturally work undertaken in the ground carries a degree of "unknown" and potentially the risk of claims for "unforeseen" works. Of course, professionals in the sector will use techniques to minimise the unknowns beforehand where possible.

Works to address subsidence could include "underpinning" for example, which would require adding additional structural support in the ground under the existing foundations. The cost for this would depend heavily on the scale and specification for the work, the location, the site and the type of property, but it would not be uncommon to encounter costs of £5,000 - £35,000+.

Render

Re-rendering work again often carries the additional associated costs of access equipment such as scaffolding. Costs can vary depending on the extent and specification of the render, and the location, but also costs can escalate if removing the existing render proves tricky. Prices could be anywhere from £2,500 - £25,000, but again these could easily be much more depending on the factors mentioned above and the size and complexity of the building itself.

Windows and doors

Replacement of windows and doors is one of the more common items of building maintenance. For your typical uPVC framed double glazed units, their life expectancy is usually around 25 years, but this can be greatly aided by routine care and maintenance in line with the manufacturer's recommendations and taking into account local climate conditions.

To replace a standard single casement uPVC framed double glazed window could be around £400, but to replace all windows and doors in a house could range from £2,000 to £25,000+ depending on quantity, specification, accessibility, building complexity and location. Wood or metal framed windows and doors would usually be much more expensive, and features such as triple glazing or self-cleaning glass would be more again.

Wall structure and wall ties

Works to address issues with the structure of walls can be costly, not least because they can be quite disruptive to other parts of the building. As a comparison imagine the mess you would create trying to change the filling in a beautifully decorated cake!

If structural building movement is noted in the survey report and works are recommended to address it, the costs for the work will vary significantly depending on the work required, extent, location, and building complexity. For example, replacement of a lintel, i.e. the structural support/beam over an opening in the wall, could require replacement of external render and internal plasterwork, redecoration, temporary structural support, potential reconfiguration of nearby services e.g. wiring, potential access equipment such as scaffolding etc, not to mention the specification, supply and installation of the new lintel/s itself. For a single lintel the cost could be anything from £500 - £3,000 depending on the factors above.

Cavity walls are a design of wall that features two walls separated by a gap. They became common throughout the UK from the early 1900's, as did the introduction of metal "wall ties". These would be placed at regular intervals into the mortar beds of the outer and inner leaves of the wall to help keep them together. Common defects associated to the ties include inadequate provision or poor installation, corrosion to the extent that they break or water travelling across the tie to the inner leaf and potentially causing damp spots inside. Issues with wall ties are largely concealed throughout the wall structure and therefore are usually initially suspected by observing symptoms of potential failure elsewhere.

Work to address cavity wall tie issues can range from relatively straight forward drilling in of new ties, to removal of the external leaf of the affected wall and rebuilding, all depending on the issue and the extent of any damage that has arisen because of it. As with foundations there is a risk that some unforeseen works could be encountered even with the aid of cameras to see inside the cavity beforehand. Again depending on the quantity, specification, complexity, access and location, costs could range from £400 - £10,000 + .

Rot

Rotting of timbers usually comes in two forms, wet rot and dry rot. Neither are particularly pleasant nor welcome in a house. They occur when timbers organically decay due to being persistently damp. Some timbers, especially older woodwork, can be more susceptible to it.

- Wet rot; Tends to occur in isolated locations where there is a high concentration of water, such as a leak for example. Moisture content in the timber is usually 50% plus. It is advisable to always address the cause of the leak first and then clean off any organic growth to the surface and allow the timber to dry out. If the timber has been badly affected, it is best to replace the damaged section.

- Dry rot; This does not occur in entirely dry conditions as the name might imply. It requires approximately 20% moisture content in the timbers to start off. Warmer temperatures, ideally 20°-30°, with high humidity and poor ventilation, (similar conditions to where you might find condensation on windows), will also improve the conditions for it growing and spreading. Unlike wet rot, dry rot will spread organically and can travel behind plasterwork and through masonry for example, even where there is no water source, potentially making it more difficult to spot and trace than wet rot. In severe cases it could even travel to neighbouring attached properties. Timbers can appear in an average condition, but beneath the surface they can be brittle and crumble. It is advisable to gain professional advice in the diagnosis and treatment of dry rot. Addressing the cause of the moisture is important and usually repair will require complete replacement of suspected affected timbers. If left untreated dry rot can travel and affect entire areas of structural timbers e.g. suspended floors/roof structures. Therefore, the costs to treat dry rot are usually higher than wet rot. Given the disruptive nature of works particularly if the rot has travelled e.g. behind plasterwork, costs can easily be in the thousands.

Electrics and heating

When it comes to building services costs are generally more predictable. Naturally as buildings age technical components wear and safety and efficiency standards increase, so that even working electrical and heating installations can become obsolete. A qualified electrician or engineer will be able to advise on how soon you are likely to need to replace service elements/installations.

The inconvenience of electrics or heating/hot water systems failing when you are living in the property means that many people choose to modernise them before this event occurs. Costs can vary significantly depending on location, size of property, complexity of building and specification of the system but often prices are between £3,000 - £12,000+ for a full rewire, and £3,500 - £15,000+ for a new heating system.

Drainage

Another element of the building which is usually concealed; suspected issues with drainage will usually require further investigation by, for example, a CCTV survey to understand the cause and specify a repair. Defects could include cracked pipes, a poorly designed and specified drainage system, poor quality materials or defective alterations. All of these have the potential to cause blockages or leaks which are particularly unpleasant if dealing with foul drainage i.e. toilet waste. Repairs to drainage systems have the potential to be quite disruptive, and depending on the location, specification, complexity and scale of the job, costs could vary from £300 - £15,000+.

Deleterious materials, invasive species, spray foam insulation, defective cavity insulation, etc.

A survey could flag up more specialist issues which require further investigation and treatment. These could include:

- Suspected deleterious materials i.e. materials which could cause harm or damage e.g. asbestos, high-alumina cement (HAC), certain types of cladding.

- Invasive biological species e.g. Japanese Knotweed, giant hogweed, Himalayan balsam.

- Spray foam insulation; something which some mortgage companies have become more sensitive to and which the RICS has recently released specific guidance on.

- Houses of non-traditional construction – especially certain types of post-war era houses identified in the Housing Defects Act 1984 which were system built and "designated defective".

- Insulation which has been retrospectively installed to wall cavities but is now defective.

It is not possible to provide an indication of cost to address these issues since their effect, extent and treatment, (or non-treatment), method will vary significantly, however given their specialist nature, works tend to be costly.

Boundary issues

These issues could be a disagreement with a neighbour over the position of a wall or even troublesome neighbours who could in theory de-value the property by putting prospective buyers off. Issues with boundaries could cost you nothing or they could cost you thousands, there really is such a wide range of scenarios that are difficult to estimate without the details of the specific circumstances. As with other aspects of life, if legal representation is required costs can escalate further. Boundary issues may not be immediately obvious and could go undetected by a surveyor. A seller is legally obliged to disclose disputes or complaints regarding the property on the "Property Information Form" (TA6) which will be provided to your solicitor. It is however wise to also try and do your own research early to unearth potential red flags, for example speaking to the owners, solicitors, and even neighbours if this is an option, to gauge potential indicators of an issue.

Obtaining prices

If you are planning on gaining prices for the work required, in some areas, it is not uncommon to come across contractors who refuse or request payment for providing a quote for a house that you do not yet own. This should be clarified and disclosed before instruction. Some points to note:

- When obtaining prices for undertaking work remember to obtain quotes from a few different contractors before deciding to go ahead.

- Be sure to note the difference between receiving "quotes" and "estimates". Quotes are an offer to do a piece of work for a specific price. An estimate on the other hand is just that; an approximate indication of how much the work could cost, and is not binding, but will vary depending on the contractor's interpretation of "reasonableness". In the construction industry the two terms are used quite fluidly and often customers do not notice or are unaware of the implications.

- Ensure you understand exactly what the quote does and doesn't include, e.g. materials, access equipment and VAT, and the payment terms e.g. full payment on completion or partial payment on completion of key milestones. It is sensible to retain some of the payment until the work is completed e.g. It is common practice to retain 5% of the agreed project price until all snagging items are satisfactorily completed.

- Make sure the contractor comes recommended and you are confident about their credibility. You could research them online, including reading past customer reviews, and look up any trade association memberships they may claim to have, or recommended trader schemes. The local authority Trading Standards department may be another useful resource.

- Depending on the work type and scale you may find that appointing a professional to procure the works and draw up contracts is more suitable. If you are unsure take professional advise as to the best course of action.

38. WHAT IS RISING DAMP?

There are entire books which could be written from many different perspectives on the subject of rising damp, hence it claiming its own "Tip" in this book.

Rising damp is defined as a form of moisture ingress that occurs when groundwater travels up through the walls of a building by capillary action – i.e. it is absorbed into the walls; like a dry paper towel held lightly in contact with a water spill. Symptoms typically are found at low level above the ground floor. Fortunately, the introduction of "damp-proof courses" (DPCs), essentially a barrier to prevent water travel, became common place in the early 1900s and advancements in materials meant that more effective membranes started to be used in the later part of the century. Symptoms of suspected rising damp are rarely a problem in buildings less than approx. 40 years old.

There are those who claim that the entire concept of rising damp is a myth, but we are not here to debate the robustness of research into the subject. Often it is the case however that the term "rising damp" is too liberally used to describe the cause of an issue which in fact could be because of some other building defect or combination of defects, for example defective nearby drainage or incompatible building materials. As a home buyer therefore, it is in this respect that you are encouraged to think critically about reports of rising damp, to question and understand its possible diagnosis and to evaluate any possible remediation if necessary. It is also worth bearing in mind that even if you are not too worried about it, it could be raised as an issue by another surveyor if you ever come to sell the house, which could put prospective buyers off.

There are many ways to deal with suspected rising damp and associated symptoms, but it will be specific to the property and the site in which it is located, and again you are encouraged not to rush into quick fix solutions. It is sensible to take the impartial advice of an RICS Chartered Building Surveyor and be mindful of taking just the recommendations made by those who may have a vested interest in you following it, e.g. by undertaking the work recommended.

39. WHAT IS PENETRATING DAMP?

While we are on the subject of damp (see Tip 38 and 40), it would make sense to discuss the term "penetrating damp" which you may find in a building survey report, along with recommendations to address it. It is essentially symptoms of water ingress inside the building which are believed to be penetrating through the exterior envelope of the building, i.e. coming from the outside in through walls, windows, roofs etc, as opposed to an internal plumbing leak for example, or rising damp from the ground.

It is wise not to get too hung up on the terminology. This is not a label attached to your building for ever more, is it simply a more concise way of describing that because of something on the outside of the building water is managing to make its way inside, the symptoms of which, i.e. staining, mould etc can be unwelcome.

It is important to treat the cause of the penetrating damp, not simply the symptoms themselves. The individual building and location will determine the many potential reasons and complexity of addressing them. More common reasons include;

- Leaking rainwater gutters and downpipes
- Opportunity for water entry around windows and door frames
- Poor condition of render
- Poor condition of joints to exposed masonry i.e. "pointing" to brickwork/stonework
- Cracked masonry
- Faulty roof coverings

Often the causes of penetrating damp symptoms are easier to diagnose than other forms of damp and may be identified and addressed by people with practical experience of buildings. However, they can on occasion be more specialist or comprise a combination of issues and if symptoms are persisting an RICS Chartered Building Surveyor will be able to investigate and recommend an appropriate cause of action. In the longer-term good building maintenance will be the most effective way of keeping symptoms of penetrating damp at bay.

40. DAMP OR CONDENSATION AND MOULD?

There is often some confusion around the terminology of damp and condensation in houses, and to further confuse things mould is often referred to interchangeably too.

Mould spores are naturally everywhere both inside and outside, but when the right environment presents itself, such as those conditions which accompany damp and condensation, the spores can grow into a visible fungus. Mould spores must land on wet/damp surfaces for it to grow. They could form into black, green and white patches, and in severe cases can affect air quality inside which could ultimately affect people's health.

It is important to note that in a house condensation could manifest anywhere where the conditions are right; usually where warm moist air comes into contact with a cold surface.

Persistent condensation/moist surfaces can often be found to corners of rooms, especially upper outside wall corners, where air circulation is less and surfaces are colder. It is also not uncommon on bathroom ceilings and walls where high levels of moisture are in the air, and in utility rooms and kitchens where appliances, cooking and washing release the most moisture.

Upstairs, warm moist air from the bathroom can rush out and settle on colder surfaces in the other rooms, particularly if the bathroom door is left open after using the shower or bath.

It is not uncommon to find issues with condensation in properties that are overcrowded or contain a lot of things, since this can limit air circulation, and more people produce more moisture into the air.

Linguistically, condensation on a surface could be referred to as damp, in the same way that you may describe damp hair, a damp towel or the ground is too damp to sit on. However, in the context of buildings, what is usually meant by damp is that water is coming into the property from the outside somehow (see Tips 38 and 39).

It is fair to say that condensation can cause a "damp environment", but it would not be uncommon to find, especially landlords and tenants, in a debate around whether a house is damp, (potentially the landlord's problem), or whether the area is subject to persistent condensation, (potentially a user issue). In fact, it can often be a blend of both and there may be some crossed wires around the terminology and the causes and remedies.

Walls and ceilings that are damp from water ingress from the outside, will likely be colder. This can provide more favourable conditions for condensation to form on their surface, and therefore damp, (i.e. water ingress), and condensation are found together. Persistent damp can also contribute to the amount of moisture in the air inside the building and again this can contribute to condensation.

Symptoms of damp and condensation can have similar characteristics in that they both might affect the surface decorations, and the surfaces might feel slightly wet to the touch. Both require addressing whether they are found in isolation or together.

Reduce condensation
- Improve ventilation; ensure that moisture generating activities such as showering and cooking are accompanied with a route to

extract the warm moist air from the inside environment. Opening windows and trickle vents or ensuring extractor fans are present and running is essential.

- Increase the temperature of cold surfaces; adding insulation and keeping the house at a consistent temperature can help with this.

- Reduce or contain the moisture; for example, keeping the bathroom door closed, putting lids on pots and avoiding things which will generate more humidity in a room such as drying clothes on radiators or racks.

- Removing condensation; where water droplets do form on surfaces it is advisable to wipe them down to help avoid persistent moisture on surfaces forming into mould.

Reduce damp symptoms

- Building maintenance; ensure that good building maintenance is carried out and external repairs are addressed e.g. leaking rainwater goods/windows, defective render/brickwork pointing.

- Reduce groundwater; keep external ground levels abutting the building below internal floor levels (with the exception of basements of course), ensure drainage is free flowing and allowing water to efficiently run away from the building, consider adding additional land drainage where the ground adjacent to the building is waterlogged.

- Avoid holding water against the building; avoid storing lots of items against the walls of the building or having dense plants growing up the walls. Where structures e.g. sheds are attached to the outside walls, ensure that correct "flashings" for example have been installed to ensure water can't become trapped in the joint between the shed and the house.

Causes of condensation are often easier to diagnose than other building issues and may be identified and addressed by people with practical experience of buildings. However, they can on occasion be more complex or comprise a combination of issues, such as damp, and if symptoms are persisting an RICS Chartered Building Surveyor will be able to investigate and recommend an appropriate cause of action.

In the longer-term, a combination of good building maintenance and user practises, will be the most effective way of reducing the risk of damp, condensation and mould growth.

41. WHAT IS RADON?

Radon is a naturally occurring radioactive gas that can be found in buildings. It is produced by the decay of the small amounts of uranium, which is present naturally in all rocks and soils. Radon gas is invisible, odourless, and tasteless, making it impossible to detect without specific testing.

Why is radon a consideration when buying a house?

Health

- Studies have shown that increased exposure to radon increases your risk of lung cancer.

- Whilst we are all exposed to radiation from natural and man-made sources, just 20Bq m^{-3}, i.e. the average radon level in UK homes, gives us half of our exposure to all radiation sources.

Location

- Certain areas of the UK have higher natural levels of radon, particularly in regions with granite or other types of rocks that have higher uranium content. This includes parts of Cornwall, Devon, Somerset, Derbyshire, Northamptonshire, and parts of Scotland and Wales.

- The UK Government and Public Health England (PHE) have identified these areas as "radon-affected areas." In these areas, it is recommended that homes be tested for radon.

Testing and mitigation

- Homeowners in radon-affected areas or those concerned about radon levels can order a radon test kit online from the UK Health Security Agency for around £55. The kit typically involves placing detectors in the property for three months to measure the average radon levels. This is because radon levels can vary over time.

- If a home's radon level exceeds the recommended "action level" then steps ought to be taken to reduce it. Reducing radon levels in a home can involve simple measures such as improving ventilation or more comprehensive steps like installing a radon sump system, which extracts radon from beneath the building and vents it outside.

Legal

- When buying or selling a home in a radon-affected area, the presence of radon is a standard consideration, and it may be raised during the conveyancing process.

- In areas known to have higher radon levels, new buildings are often required to be constructed with radon-resistant features, such as radon barriers or sumps, to prevent the gas from accumulating inside.

42. WHAT ABOUT ASBESTOS?

Asbestos is a group of naturally occurring fibrous minerals that were widely used in the construction industry but were finally banned in the UK in 1999. The fibres were blending into various materials from boards to plasters and vinyls to drainpipes.

The reason asbestos fibres were used so extensively was due to their durability, fire resistance, and insulating properties. However, asbestos is now known to be highly dangerous if its fibres are inhaled, leading to serious/critical health risks including lung cancer, asbestosis and mesothelioma.

Asbestos-containing materials (ACMs) are still present in many older buildings, and the HSE (Health and Safety Executive) advises that any buildings built/refurbished pre-2000 should be assumed to contain some asbestos. Should asbestos be found it can be removed, (in compliance with statutory methods), left in place and managed or encapsulated, depending on its type and location among other factors. An asbestos surveyor can provide recommendations in this respect.

When selling a property, the presence of asbestos must be disclosed by the vendors if known. The presence of asbestos could affect the property valuation and be a reason for further negotiation of the purchase price or choosing not to buy the house.

In dealing with asbestos homeowners who live in their property do not have the same legal obligations as landlords and other building owners. Nevertheless, it is important they select qualified and reputable tradespeople to carry out any building work who can flag up if an asbestos survey is required. A survey is the most reliable way to determine if asbestos is present in the property.

If you are a DIY enthusiast or rely on the help of family and friends with repairs and improvements to your house, then it would be wise to have an asbestos survey anyway even though you may not be legally obliged.

A specialist asbestos consulting firm can give you a quote for one of the following:

- Management Survey: A standard survey to locate the presence and condition of asbestos-containing materials (ACMs) that could be disturbed during normal occupancy, including minor maintenance work.

- Refurbishment and Demolition Survey (R&D Survey): A more thorough survey required before any significant renovation or demolition work. This survey is more intrusive and designed to locate all ACMs in the building. If you haven't yet bought the house carrying out intrusive investigations such as damage to plasterwork will require special consent from the seller, and you may find they are resistant to this.

43. WHAT IF THERE'S CRACKS?

There are many different cracks in buildings, and they are indicative that some movement, even if only to surface plasters, has taken place. Many are superficial and can benefit from simple repair; however, some are symptomatic of more significant structural issues. The latter can have implications in terms of repair costs, mortgageability, insurance and property value and saleability.

It is worth remembering that the cracks are the symptom of a cause and not the cause itself. Causes can be wide ranging from differential thermal movement between contrasting building materials, to root damage or ground structure.

Causes can be broadly defined as follows:

- Temperature-induced size changes
- Moisture-induced size changes
- Chemically-induced size changes
- Foundation movement
- Mechanical damage or impact
- Vibration damage
- Indirect damage
- Frost damage

In all cases if you are buying a home with cracks, it is wise to instruct a Chartered Building Surveyor, or Structural Engineer to investigate. If you are having an RICS Level 2 or 3 survey carried out anyway (see Tip 3), the cracks themselves are likely to be picked up during the inspection, but it is always worth mentioning your concerns to the surveyor in advance of their visit.

Industry guidance defines five categories of damage. In general, categories 0, 1 and 2 with crack widths up to 5 mm can be considered 'aesthetic' issues that require redecoration only. Categories 3 and 4 can generally be regarded as 'serviceability' issues, in that they affect the weathertightness of the building and the operation of windows and doors. Category 5 presents 'stability' issues and is likely to require structural intervention. It is important not to rely too heavily on these categories however, as the collection or position of a combination of cracks, even smaller ones, could be diagnosed by a professional as indicative of more severe underlying issues which need addressing.

For many types of more serious cracking, recommendations will include monitoring the cracks over time to assess whether they are stable or worsening. This would include measuring crack widths and observing any new cracks.

The appropriate remedy depends on the severity and cause of the cracking. While cosmetic cracks can be easily repaired, the presence of structural cracks may require significant interventions like underpinning or reinforcement and therefore may prompt a buyer to further negotiate on the purchase price, or they may even decide to withdraw from the purchase.

SEARCHES AND SERVICES

44. WHAT IF IT'S IN AN AREA OF FLOOD RISK?

It is important to know if the house you are buying is in an area of flood risk as it can have a significant impact on insurance, lenders, the property value and saleability in future, and of course your quality of life in the event of flooding. You should be factoring these points into the price you are paying for the property and be aware of how the various issues could affect you in the longer term.

Flooding can come from various sources including:

- Rivers (fluvial flooding)
- Sea/Coastal
- Surface water (pluvial flooding)
- Groundwater – where the water table rises

Check your flood risk

- Use the Environment Agency's/Natural Resources Wales' flood map service to check whether the property is in a flood risk area.
- Flood risk categories or zones indicate if you are in a low, medium, or high risk of flooding from rivers, seas, and surface water.
- Searches initiated by your solicitor/conveyancer may reveal more detailed information about the flood risk of the property (see Tip 52).

Flood risk assessment and prevention

- You can commission a professional flood risk survey to understand specific vulnerabilities and what measures can be taken to reduce risk.

- Consider installing preventative measures such as flood barriers, air brick covers, or non-return valves on drains to avoid water entering the building.

- Adapt the home with more compatible materials such as floor tiles instead of carpets. You could also raise electrical sockets and appliances above potential flood levels.

Sign up for flood alerts

Register for flood warnings with the Environment Agency / Natural Resources Wales, which provide real-time alerts and guidance during heavy rainfall or when river levels are rising.

Purchase flood insurance

- Insurance for properties in flood risk areas is likely to be higher. Investigate this before purchasing the property.

- Ensure your home insurance covers flood damage. Some properties at high risk may need specialist insurance under the "Flood Re" scheme, which helps make flood insurance available and more affordable.

- Review insurance policies for specific coverage, as not all standard home insurance policies cover flood damage.

- Ask the current owners who they insure their home with and what the policy covers.

Create a flood plan

Develop a plan to protect your new home and family in case of a flood. Include steps such as moving valuables and electrical appliances to higher floors, turning off gas, water, and electricity, and knowing how to evacuate safely.

Consider long-term defences

Engage with local councils and flood action groups to support community-level flood defences like raised embankments, levees, or improved drainage systems.

Use landscaping techniques like creating absorbent surfaces (gravel instead of tarmac) to improve drainage around your property.

45. HOW DO I TRANSFER OR CONNECT UTILITIES? E.G. WATER, DRAINAGE, ELECTRIC, GAS, OIL, BROADBAND, PHONE

When moving house there are several key utilities and services you'll need to transfer or connect, including water, drainage, electricity, gas, oil, broadband, and phone.

Water and drainage

- Contact your current water supplier and inform them of your move. You'll need to provide your moving date, final meter reading (if applicable), and new address for the final bill.

- If you're moving to a new region, contact the local water supplier (e.g., Thames Water, Severn Trent, Dwr Cymru) to register the property under your name. They will set up a new account for you and advise if the property is metered.

- Sewerage services are often provided by the same company that supplies water, but in some areas, it might be a different provider. Contact the sewerage company to notify them of your move.

Electricity and gas (if applicable)

- Inform your current gas and electricity provider of your move, providing the final meter readings on moving day. Ask them to issue your final bill and confirm if they can supply your new property.

- If you want to stay with the same supplier, contact them to arrange the transfer of your service. If you're switching providers, shop around for the best rates and notify the new company.

- Upon moving in, take meter readings to ensure you are billed correctly from the start. If the property has a prepayment meter, you may want to switch it to a standard meter.

Oil (if applicable)

- If your current property is heated by oil, inform your supplier that you are moving. Arrange for any remaining oil to be used or sold to the new occupant.

- If the new house is also oil-heated, find out the oil tank size and location, and contact a local oil supplier to set up deliveries. You might want to arrange an initial delivery if the tank is low. Speak to the current owner to find out which supplier they use and the usual rate.

Broadband and phone

- Use provider services to check broadband availability at your new home. Ensure you know whether fibre, satellite, standard, or cable broadband is available.

- If your current provider covers the new area, you may wish to contact them to arrange transferring your contract. If they don't, check if you are within a penalty-free period to cancel or switch to a new provider.

- New broadband connections may take up to two weeks, especially if an engineer visit is required for cable installation.

Phone line

- Traditional land lines under the "PSTN" services will be fully retired by the end of 2025. You will be switched to, (if not already), or given a digital service instead via a Voice over Internet Protocol (VoIP) phone, which operates through your broadband connection. Speak to your service provider if you want to keep an existing phone number.

General

- Notify providers early. Inform all utility and service providers of your moving date as soon as possible and at least two weeks in advance. Many providers require notice, and this will help ensure continuity of service.

- Take meter readings on the day you move out and the day you move into your new home and take photos of the meters to ensure accurate billing.

- You can also use the Royal Mail's redirection service to forward any remaining mail to your new address for a specified period. This grants you a little more time to see if there is anyone you haven't yet notified.

- If the thought of doing all this seems daunting, don't despair. In recent years several companies have emerged who can help take care of this, one of life's more tedious admin tasks. A simple online search will list come of the companies who will be more than happy to help.

46. WHAT DOCUMENTATION COULD COME WITH A HOUSE?

When you buy a house certain documents could be provided by the seller and through the legal conveyancing process. These documents help ensure the property's legal ownership, its condition, and your responsibilities as the new owner. Here's a breakdown of the documentation you could expect to receive.

Official Copy of the Register, Title Plan and Transfer Deed (TR1)

- These are essential and are the official legal documents proving ownership of the property. They also identify any restrictions or covenants that may apply to the property. They are recorded digitally with the Land Registry.

- If the house you're buying only has paper Title Deeds/Deed of Conveyance, it likely means it's unregistered with the Land Registry. The solicitors will need to verify the deeds and apply for first registration, which will mean the process usually takes longer. Once registered, the property will have a title number, and future transactions will be recorded electronically.

Mortgage deed (if applicable)

- The deed secures the mortgage loan by using the property as collateral, giving the lender the right to take possession of the property if the borrower doesn't repay the money lent.

- Includes details such as the parties involved, amount of loan, interest rate, repayment schedule and length of mortgage.

- The deed is usually registered with the Land Registry.

Seller's Property Information Form (also known as PIF/TA6)

- A comprehensive document completed by the seller providing important information about the property, such as boundary disputes, planning permissions, and whether the property has ever been flooded.

Fittings and Contents Form (TA10)

- This form lists what is included in the sale, such as fixtures, fittings, and appliances (e.g. kitchen units, carpets, light fixtures).

- It helps you to know exactly what is staying in the house and what the seller will take with them, so that you can start planning for any essentials you might need to get such as curtains/blinds.

- If you agree anything verbally with the seller, such as appliances they might leave, it is vital that this is communicated in writing with the solicitors. If the solicitors aren't aware and haven't confirmed agreement of this with each other, then you will have little course for redress in the event that a verbal agreement isn't honoured.

Energy Performance Certificate (EPC) (see Tip 51)

- An EPC rates the energy efficiency of the property on a scale from A (most efficient) to G (least efficient).

- It helps you understand how energy-efficient the property is and what energy-saving improvements might be needed.

Building Regulation Certificates and Planning Permissions

- Certificates that show eligible work carried out on the property, such as extensions or structural changes, complied with building regulations. This may also include planning permissions for alterations or additions to the property.

- Ensures that significant modifications made to the property were done legally and to required standards, reducing the risk of future legal issues.

- Certificates could also include FENSA certificates for window and door installations since 2002 (see Tip 48), and HETAS certificates for solid fuel appliances/stoves or open fires installed since 2005.

Gas Safety Certificate (if applicable)

- For properties with gas installations, a Gas Safety Certificate confirms that the gas systems and appliances were inspected by a qualified engineer and are considered safe.

Electrical Installation Condition Report (EICR) / Electrical Installation Certificate (EIC)

- An inspection report on the electrical wiring and installations in the property.

- Certifies whether the electrical systems in the house are safe and comply with current standards; particularly important for older homes.

Boiler service records

- Documentation that shows the boiler has been serviced regularly.
- Demonstrates that the heating system is in good working order and helps reduce unexpected repair costs.

Guarantees and warranties

- Documentation for any guarantees or warranties on elements such as the roof, windows, damp-proofing, or recent building work.
- If it's a new home, there may be a Professional Consultant's Certificate or a Structural Warranty such as NHBC. (see Tip 60)

Leasehold/Freehold information (if applicable)

- If the property is leasehold (see Tip 57), you will need the Leasehold Agreement and documents detailing the lease terms, any ground rent, and any service charges, usually in the form of a Leasehold Information Form TA7 from the seller and a Management Pack/LPE1 from the Landlord or managing agent.
- Deed of Covenant, (if required by the lease); a legal promise by the leaseholder to follow lease terms.
- License to Assign (if required by the lease), where the leaseholder needs the freeholder's permission to sell the property.

- For freehold properties (see Tip58), any information about shared amenities, service charges or restrictions (such as in private developments) should be included.

Indemnity insurance (if applicable)

- A type of insurance policy taken out to cover any legal issues that might arise due to missing documentation or historical issues (e.g. lack of building regulation approval).

- Provides protection against potential future legal challenges.

Stamp Duty Land Tax receipt in England (SDLT5 certificate)

- Provided via your solicitor following payment of SDLT.

- Confirms the tax liability for the property, (above a certain value), has been paid, (see Tip 2).

47. WHAT IF THERE'S NO BUILDING REGULATIONS FOR ALTERATIONS/EXTENSIONS?

Building regulations exist to ensure that work carried out on a property, such as extensions or significant alterations, complies with safety and performance standards. The absence of these certificates can introduce both legal and safety risks.

If the house you are buying lacks a building regulation completion certificate or any evidence of an application for extensions or alterations, there are some actions you can take.

Request retrospective approval

- Retrospective building regulation approval can be applied for, also known as a regularisation certificate. This involves contacting the local council's building control department, who will inspect the work to check if it complies with current standards.

- The council may request that parts of the building be opened up for inspection (e.g. removing plaster or flooring to check structural elements). If the work does not comply, they may require corrective actions to bring it up to standard.

- There could be substantial costs if the work does not meet current regulations and needs to be altered or redone to achieve compliance.

Indemnity insurance

- If you are unable to obtain a building regulation certificate or do not want to seek retrospective approval, you may opt to purchase indemnity insurance. This insurance covers you financially against enforcement action by the local council for any lack of building regulation approval.

- This type of insurance can usually only be obtained if no one has contacted the local council about the missing certificate. If they are already aware of the issue, indemnity insurance will not be available.

- The cost of indemnity insurance typically ranges from a few hundred to a thousand pounds, depending on the property size and the extent of the alterations.

- Indemnity insurance covers only legal costs and does not address safety concerns. If there are any safety issues (e.g., faulty wiring or structural problems), the buyer remains responsible for any remedial work required.

Negotiate with the seller

- If there is no building regulation certificate, you can ask the seller to reduce the purchase price to account for the risks and potential costs of rectifying any non-compliant work.

- You can request that the seller obtains a regularisation certificate before completion or provide indemnity insurance at their expense.

Check with a Structural Engineer or Surveyor

- Before proceeding, you should commission a survey to assess whether the work is sound. A surveyor or structural engineer can provide insight into whether the alterations pose any risks.

- The absence of a building regulation certificate may hide underlying problems like substandard construction, poor-quality materials, or safety hazards such as improper electrical or plumbing work, (a qualified electrician or plumber may be required in these cases). A detailed survey may require some intrusive investigations such as cutting open plasterwork to view walls – this will require homeowner consent, and you could face resistance on this.

Risks

- Mortgage reassessment – Your lenders could reassess their offer and require certain conditions to be met or even reduce their loan offer or withdraw it.

- Enforcement action - If the local authority is aware of the issue they have the power to serve an enforcement notice for unauthorised work that does not meet building regulations, potentially requiring remedial work or, in extreme cases, demolition of the unauthorised alterations.

- Safety risks - Work that has not been checked by building control may not meet modern safety standards. For example, electrical installations might not comply with current wiring regulations, posing a fire hazard, or structural alterations could compromise the building's stability.

- Impact on resale - The lack of building regulation approval can make it harder to sell the property in the future. Buyers, (and lenders), may be reluctant to purchase a property without the necessary certificates or may try and negotiate significant price reductions.

- Increased insurance premiums - Some home insurance companies may increase premiums or refuse to cover properties with unauthorised alterations, as the risk of damage or failure is higher.

48. WHAT IS A FENSA CERTIFICATE?

A FENSA certificate is a document issued to homeowners as proof that any replacement windows and doors installed, (since 2002), in their property comply with current Building Regulations in England and Wales. FENSA (Fenestration Self-Assessment Scheme) is a government-authorised scheme that certifies that the work was carried out by an installer registered with FENSA, ensuring it meets the required standards for energy efficiency, safety, and proper installation. By having a FENSA certificate, a separate Building Regulation Approval for windows and doors wouldn't usually be required, although if the property is a listed building separate legislation applies and conservation officer consent may have been required.

This document is particularly important when selling your property on again, as buyers will often ask for proof that any work done was compliant with regulations.

What do I need if the sellers don't have a FENSA Certificate?

- Building Regulation approval - A compliance certificate stating the works meet regulations.

- Competent Person Scheme alternatives - Other schemes, like Certass also issue certificates confirming compliance with Building Regulations for window and door installations.

- Retrospective inspection - If neither a FENSA certificate, (or approved alternative), nor a Building Regulations compliance certificate is available, a retrospective inspection from your local council may be required and a Regularisation Certificate issued.

- Indemnity insurance - If the seller it not obtaining retrospective approval, you may be able to obtain indemnity insurance. This type of insurance protects you financially if enforcement action is taken due to the lack of building regulation approval or a FENSA certificate. It is important to note that indemnity insurance may only be available if no enforcement action has already been initiated or if the local council has not been notified about the lack of approval.

49. WHAT IF THERE'S NO PLANNING PERMISSION FOR ALTERATIONS/EXTENSIONS?

If there is no planning permission for alterations or extensions to a house you are buying, there are some things you can do, but it's vital to understand the risks involved. Lack of planning permission, where it was required, can lead to enforcement action by the local authority, mortgage offer withdrawal, and it may affect your ability to sell the property in the future.

Check if Planning Permission was required

- In some cases, certain alterations or extensions may not require formal planning permission. These are called Permitted Development Rights and apply to specific types of work, such as small rear extensions or loft conversions, within certain limits.

- You can check with the local planning authority (LPA) to confirm whether the work falls under permitted development or should have required planning permission.

Obtain retrospective Planning Permission

- If the work needed planning permission but it was never applied for, you can submit a retrospective planning application for a Lawful Development Certificate. If the work complies with current regulations, permission may still be granted.

- If retrospective permission is refused, you may be required to reverse the alterations or demolish any unauthorised extensions.

Indemnity insurance

- You may be able to purchase indemnity insurance to protect you against enforcement action, that is if the local authority hasn't already been alerted to the lack of planning permission and disputes have not already been raised. This type of insurance covers legal costs if the council requires you to undo or modify the alterations.

- Indemnity insurance is only available if no contact has been made with the council regarding the unauthorised work. It won't cover the cost of making changes to comply with planning regulations if enforcement action is taken.

Issues

- Local councils can take enforcement action within time limits of 4-10 years depending on when the development was completed. It is important to gain professional advice on this, for example from a Planning Consultant.

- The lack of planning permission can complicate or even prevent the sale of the property in the future, as buyers and mortgage lenders may be hesitant to proceed with the purchase.

- Some mortgage lenders may refuse to lend on a property with unauthorised extensions or alterations, and insurance providers may increase premiums or refuse coverage.

50. WHAT IF THE LOFT CONVERSION IS NOT "OFFICIAL"?

Many older houses in particular, have had loft/attic conversions, (the terms are used interchangeably), carried out without gaining the necessary statutory consents e.g. planning permission, (if required), and building regulation approval. If this is the case for the house you're buying, there are some steps you can take to manage the risk.

Check if Planning Permission was required

Some loft conversions may not require planning permission if they fall under Permitted Development Rights. This typically includes loft conversions that don't exceed certain volume limits and don't significantly alter the roof structure. However, if the conversion involves significant alterations like dormer windows or raising the roof, planning permission may be necessary.

Local Authority Check: Contact the local authority to check whether the loft conversion was within the limits of Permitted Development or if it should have had planning permission. Be aware that alerting them to the issue could remove the opportunity to gain indemnity insurance for the issue.

Building Regulations approval

Even if planning permission wasn't required, all loft conversions should meet building regulation requirements to ensure the work is structurally sound and safe. This includes fire safety measures (such as fire-resistant materials and escape routes), structural integrity, proper insulation, and adequate ventilation.

If the loft conversion lacks building regulation approval, you can apply for retrospective approval through the local authority (see Tip 47). This may involve an inspection by a building control officer. They might ask for part of the work to be exposed (e.g. lifting floorboards or removing plasterboard) to assess compliance. Bear in mind that if you go down this route you may be required to significantly upgrade parts of the building which could be costly, and it could eliminate the possibility of obtaining indemnity insurance.

Indemnity insurance

If you are not obtaining retrospective approval, you may be able to obtain indemnity insurance. This type of insurance protects you financially if the local authority takes enforcement action due to the lack of building regulation or planning approval. However, this insurance will only cover legal costs and does not address safety concerns or remedy non-compliant work. It is important to note that indemnity insurance is only available if no enforcement action has already been initiated or if the local council has not been notified about the lack of approval.

Negotiate with the seller

If the loft conversion does not have the necessary approval, you could consider negotiating with the seller to reduce the purchase price to cover potential future costs of obtaining approval, making necessary alterations, or even dismantling non-compliant work. You could also request that the seller applies for and obtains retrospective approval before completing the sale, but in a competitive market you could well face push back on this.

Get a survey (see Tip 3)

An RICS surveyor or an experienced Structural Engineer can assess whether the loft conversion is structurally sound and safe. This is particularly important if there is no building regulation approval, as it could uncover issues such as inadequate structural support, poor insulation, or fire hazards. If significant issues are found, you may need to factor in the cost of remedial work to bring the conversion up to standard. A detailed survey may require some intrusive investigations such as cutting open boxing in to view beams – this will require homeowner consent and again you could face push back on this.

Risks

- Safety issues - If the loft conversion hasn't been inspected by building control, there may be safety issues, such as inadequate structural support, fire risks, or improper insulation. These can lead to significant future repair costs or safety hazards for occupants.

- Legal and financial risks – If the local authority is aware of the breach, they have the authority to take enforcement action if the loft conversion doesn't comply with building regulations. This could involve requiring you to make alterations or, in extreme cases, undo the work.

- The absence of planning permission and/or building regulation approval could make it harder to sell the property in the future, as future buyers or their solicitors may raise concerns over the unauthorised work. It may also give buyers scope to try and negotiate a price reduction to cover the potential risks and costs.

- Some mortgage lenders may be hesitant to lend on properties with unauthorised conversions, and home insurance providers may increase premiums or refuse to cover a property that hasn't been approved.

51. WHAT ARE ENERGY PERFORMANCE CERTIFICATES (EPC'S)?

An Energy Performance Certificate, or EPC as it is most commonly referred to, is a document that provides an assessment of a property's energy efficiency and environmental impact, rated on a scale from A (most efficient) to G (least efficient). It is required for properties that are being sold, rented, or constructed in the UK. EPCs offer information on the property's current energy use and CO_2 emissions and provide very high level recommendations for improvements to reduce energy consumption and improve efficiency.

An EPC is valid for 10 years and must be presented to prospective buyers or tenants before any transaction is finalised. The certificate also estimates potential energy savings from upgrades and highlights what the energy efficiency rating could be if these measures are implemented.

Things to note

Ensure the seller provides an EPC

- The seller is legally required to provide an EPC when you are purchasing a home. You should receive the EPC before you exchange contracts.

Review the EPC to understand energy efficiency

- As a buyer, it's essential to review the EPC to understand the energy efficiency of the property and potential future costs. This can help you plan for improvements and understand whether the home meets your energy-efficiency expectations.

- It can also affect your running costs since less efficient homes may have higher heating and electricity bills.

Factor in future improvements

- Use the EPC's recommendations to consider any energy-efficient upgrades you may want to implement after purchasing the property. If you plan to make improvements, the EPC provides an indication of what steps to take to improve energy performance.

Comply with EPC regulations

- If you plan to sell or rent the property in the future, you will need to ensure a valid EPC is available and provided to prospective buyers or tenants.

- It is reported that from December 2030 a new law will require mortgage lenders to achieve an average EPC rating of C across their domestic loans.

- From December 2035 it is expected that non-mortgage owner occupied homes will also need to have a rating of C or above.

- If you're buying a buy-to-let property, minimum EPC rating requirements already apply; landlords must ensure that their rental properties have an EPC rating of E or above. Otherwise, they may face penalties or be prohibited from renting out the property until improvements are made. It is expected however from December 2025 the bar will raise again, and new tenancies for rented houses will need to achieve a rating of C or above, with existing tenanted properties joining them by 2028.

52. WHAT ARE "SEARCHES"?

Searches are an essential part of the conveyancing process when buying a house. These searches are usually requested by the solicitor or conveyancer on behalf of the buyer/lender and are designed to uncover legal, environmental, or planning issues that may affect the property or its value. They typically take between two to six weeks, though some local authorities and organisations may process them faster, while others may take longer depending on the complexity of the search and their resources.

Local Authority Search

The local authority search provides information about the property and surrounding area from the local council. It is divided into two parts.

- LLC1 (Local Land Charges Register): This reveals any local charges or restrictions on the property, such as listed building status, conservation area restrictions, tree preservation orders, or planning agreements.

- CON29: This includes information on planning applications (past and pending), building control issues, proposed road schemes, railway developments, and any nearby contamination or hazardous risks.

Environmental Search

This search identifies environmental risks associated with the property, such as the risk of subsidence, contamination (e.g., land previously used for industrial purposes), or proximity to landfill sites.

Water and Drainage Search

This search checks if the property is connected to the public water supply and sewer system. It also identifies the location of pipes and sewers, which may affect future development.

Chancel Repair Search

This checks if the property is subject to a historic liability to contribute to the cost of repairs for the local parish church, a rare but potentially costly obligation.

Flood Risk Search

It assesses whether the property is at risk of flooding from rivers, the sea, or surface water. Properties at risk of flooding can potentially face higher insurance premiums and more expensive future repairs (see Tip 44).

53. WHAT IS A RIGHT OF WAY?

Rights of way are legal rights that allow someone (other than the homeowner) to pass through or use part of a property. All rights of way are a type of easement, so you may hear these two terms used interchangeably. These rights may impact your use of the property, and it is essential to understand them fully before proceeding with the purchase.

Types of rights of way

- Public rights of way: These are rights for the general public to pass over certain paths or roads, typically footpaths, bridleways, or byways. They may run through or adjacent to your property. Public rights of way are registered with local authorities and are generally non-negotiable.

- If a public footpath or bridleway runs through or near your property, you will have limited control over its use. You can, however, apply to divert or close a public right of way, but this can be a lengthy and complex process.

- Private rights of way: This refers to a legal right for specific individuals (often neighbouring landowners) to use part of your property, typically for access. This is common with properties that share driveways or where neighbouring properties need to cross your land to access their own.

- Private rights of way can limit your use of the affected land. For example, you may not be able to block the access, build on the land, or restrict the neighbours' use. It's important to review the terms of the right of way carefully, as it may also involve obligations like maintenance.

Check legal documentation

- Your solicitor/conveyancer should check the property title register and plan, to see if any rights of way are registered which affect the property.

- It is also worth checking for discrepancies between the Land Registry documents and the property's original deeds if available.

- Your solicitor/conveyancer will carry out a local authority search (see Tip 52), to check if any public rights of way affect the property and should also check whether there are plans for future developments that might introduce new rights of way.

Negotiating rights of way

- In some cases, it may be possible to negotiate with the holder of a private right of way to remove or modify it. This can involve legal agreements and may require compensation. However, public rights of way are harder to change and require a legal process through the local authority, which may not always succeed.

- If the right of way is beneficial to you (for example, giving you access to a shared driveway), your solicitor will ensure it is properly registered as an easement so you can legally use the path or road.

- If there is a public or private right of way over your land, it could reduce the market value or make the property less attractive to future buyers, as it may be seen as an inconvenience.

Insurance for rights of way

- If the right of way is a concern (for example, if it is undocumented or contentious), you may be able to purchase indemnity insurance. This covers legal costs, or compensation claims if there are disputes or problems with the right of way in the future. Mortgage lenders may insist upon this as a way of reducing their risk exposure.

54. WHAT IS "OVERAGE"?

An overage agreement (also known as clawback) is a provision sometimes included in property transactions, typically when buying land or a house with potential for future development or value increases. It gives the seller the right to a share of the increased value if the buyer later enhances the property or land in a way that significantly increases its market value, such as obtaining planning permission or building additional structures.

How overage works

The overage clause is triggered by specific events that increase the value of the property. Common triggers include:

- The new owner obtains planning permission for development or substantial extensions.

- The resale of the property within a certain timeframe at a higher price.

- Completion of development projects that increase the property's value.

If a trigger event occurs, the buyer (now the property owner) must pay a percentage of the increase in value to the original seller. This percentage is agreed upon at the time of the sale and documented in the overage agreement. For example, if planning permission for additional houses is obtained, the seller may be entitled to 25-50% of the additional market value of the land.

The agreement specifies how long the overage clause remains in effect. It may last for several years or even decades, depending on the terms agreed between the parties. After this period expires, the buyer is free to develop the property without paying any overage.

Key considerations

- Duration: The overage period is usually defined in the contract, often ranging from 10 to 50 years.

- Calculation: The value increase is typically calculated based on market values at the time of development, and the overage is a percentage of that uplift in value.

- Tax: Stamp Duty Land Tax/Land Transaction Tax (see Tip 27) is usually payable on the overage. Buyers can apply to HMRC to defer this until the overage has been calculated and paid.

- Registration: Overage provisions are usually registered against the title of the property, so they will bind future owners too unless explicitly released.

- Negotiation: Buyers and sellers can negotiate overage terms before the sale, including how much of the uplift in value the seller is entitled to, what triggers the overage, and how long the agreement lasts.

55. WHAT IF THERE ARE BOUNDARY ISSUES?

If you suspect or discover a boundary issue with the house you're buying, it's essential to address it before proceeding with the purchase.

Boundary issues typically arise when there is a dispute or uncertainty about the exact dividing lines between your property and your neighbours' properties. These can range from disagreements over fence placement to issues with access rights or ownership of certain land.

If there are issues it is better to resolve these before you have bought the property, when you still have the option to withdraw from the purchase or negotiate the price/terms. It is important to think long and hard about whether this is a problem you want to potentially inherit.

How to know if there is a boundary issue

- The Land Registry title plan shows the general boundaries of the property you are buying. This plan, however, is not definitive for the exact position of boundaries, as the boundaries on title plans are drawn with thick red lines, which can sometimes leave room for interpretation.

- Take ownership of cross checking the physical boundaries with the recorded boundaries yourself. Solicitors don't typically visit the house you are buying themselves, so it is possible for discrepancies to go unnoticed.

- Your conveyancer/solicitor could review the original title deeds and title plan carefully. The deeds might contain detailed information about boundary positions, fence ownership, or previous agreements.

- Ask the seller about any known boundary disputes or historical issues. They are obliged to disclose disputes, especially if it has led to formal legal action.

- If you suspect a boundary issue could be present you could consider hiring a Chartered Surveyor who specialises in land to conduct a boundary survey. They can offer a professional assessment of where the boundary lines are likely to be, based on the physical features of the property and any information in the title plan or deeds.

- If possible, you could talk to the neighbours to see if they agree on the boundary positions. Neighbours often have valuable knowledge about the history of the land or any informal agreements regarding boundaries.

What to do if there is a boundary issue

Seek legal advice

If you discover any boundary issues, speak to your solicitor immediately. They will review official documentation to determine the extent of the problem.

They may recommend obtaining a boundary agreement with the neighbours that clarifies the exact boundary and is registered with the Land Registry. You may also decide to withdraw from the purchase.

Indemnity insurance

If a minor boundary issue cannot be easily resolved, you may be able to obtain indemnity insurance. This insurance can protect you financially if claims are made by neighbours about the boundary or if legal action is taken against you regarding the boundary lines.

Risks of boundary issues

- Ongoing or unresolved boundary issues can lead to disputes with neighbours, which may result in costly legal battles.

- Properties with unresolved boundary issues may be less attractive to future buyers, reducing the value or delaying the sale.

- If a boundary dispute involves land that you believe to be part of your property, you may lose the right to use that land or be forced to move or remove structures (e.g., fences or extensions).

- Neighbourly disputes can be personally stressful. Animosity with someone who you may potentially run into every day can contribute to anxiety.

56. WHO IS THE LAND REGISTRY?

The Land Registry is a UK government agency responsible for registering the ownership of land and property in England and Wales. It maintains an official and centralised record of who owns land and property, and it has a range of services for property owners, buyers, solicitors, and mortgage lenders.

When you are buying a house, it is important to check land registry information carefully and it is worth cross referencing the title plan to the actual property for accuracy. If there are any discrepancies it is better to resolve these before you have bought it, when you still have the option to withdraw from the purchase or negotiate the price/terms.

Key features

- The Land Registry holds and updates the register of land ownership, which includes details about land, property boundaries, mortgages, restrictive covenants, (agreements which limit how the land can be used), and easements (such as rights of way).

- By registering property with the Land Registry, owners gain legal protection against claims by third parties, as the registered owner's title is guaranteed by the state.

- The Land Registry provides title plans that show general boundaries and holds copies of title deeds, which outline any conditions or restrictions attached to the property.

- They have a publicly accessible database of registered properties online where the Title register and Title Plan can be bought and downloaded. See https://www.gov.uk/search-property-information-land-registry

57. WHAT IS A LEASEHOLD?

Leasehold is a form of property ownership where you purchase the right to live in or use a property for a fixed period of time, but do not own the land on which the property stands, or potentially the building structure and communal areas in the case of flats/apartments.

Instead, the land is owned by a freeholder (sometimes called a landlord), and you are required to follow the terms of the lease during your ownership.

At the time of writing leaseholds are under political scrutiny with plans to reform the laws governing them. Experts anticipate these changes taking effect sometime in 2025 and they could notably reduce the risks for leasehold homeowners.

Buying a leasehold property usually comes with additional complexities that can add to the timescales and costs. As always, when buying a property, it is advisable to get experienced professional advice.

Key features

- Fixed term: Leaseholds typically last for a set number of years, often between 99 to 999 years, although shorter leases (e.g., 30 or 60 years) are also possible. Once the lease term expires, ownership of the property reverts to the freeholder unless you extend the lease.

- Ground rent: Leaseholders may have to pay an annual ground rent to the freeholder on demand. The amount is often specified in the lease agreement and back payments of up to 6 years can be recovered. They can also sometimes increase over time. If you have a new lease granted from the freeholder after 30th June 2022 the landlord cannot charge you anything more than a "peppercorn" ground rent, the value of which is zero. If however, you bought the lease from another leaseholder then you still have to pay in accordance with that lease.

- Service charges: Leaseholders usually have to contribute towards the upkeep of the building or communal areas, known as service charges. This can cover maintenance, repairs, insurance, and other costs associated with the management of the property (see Tips 29 and 37).

- Permission for alterations: In many cases, leaseholders need to seek permission from the freeholder to make any significant alterations or improvements to the property. Sometimes they may also require a more detailed document called a "Licence for Alterations".

- Lease extension: If the lease is running low (typically below 80 years), the property may decrease in value, and it may become harder to sell. Mortgage lenders may also be reluctant to lend against the property. In this case subject to eligibility, the leaseholder has rights which mean they can usually apply to extend the lease, though this may involve significant costs. Online lease extension calculators can give you an early indication of these.

- Apportionment: The buyer may be required to reimburse the seller for prepaid service charges and ground rent covering the period after completion.

- Buying the freehold: In some cases, leaseholders may be entitled to buy the freehold for a property from their landlord. Where this is without the landlord's agreement it is called enfranchisement. Be aware that whilst freehold is generally considered desirable to prospective buyers, freehold flats are less so because many mortgage lenders won't lend against them.

58. WHAT IS A FREEHOLD?

Freehold is a form of property ownership where you own both the property and the land it stands on outright. As a freeholder, you have full ownership of the property for an unlimited amount of time, unlike leasehold ownership, which is limited to a set number of years. Freehold ownership is the most complete form of ownership and typically applies to houses, though in some cases, it may apply to flats/apartments as well.

Some people are surprised to find that owning the freehold for a property doesn't necessarily mean you have what is called "mineral rights" to the ground underneath. By default, gas, oil, coal, gold and silver are owned by the state. Generally other minerals are owned by the freeholder unless they have been previously assigned to someone else.

Key Features

- Full ownership: As the freeholder, you own both the land and the property permanently. You have full control over it, including how it is used and modified, subject to achieving statutory consents, local laws and "Party Wall" matters with adjoining neighbours.

- No ground rent: Unlike leaseholders, freeholders do not pay ground rent to a landlord or freeholder because they own the land.

- Maintenance responsibility: As a freeholder, you are fully responsible for maintaining both the building and the land. This includes structural repairs, roof maintenance, and managing any outdoor spaces.

- No service charges or restrictions: There are usually no service charges or restrictions typically imposed by a third party, which is otherwise common with leasehold properties where you might have to adhere to the landlord's or management company's rules. The exception to this is where you may be part of a private estate or building for example and you are required to contribute to the maintenance and management of communal areas (see Tip 33).

- Easier to sell: Arguably freehold properties are generally easier and quicker to sell compared to leasehold ones, as buyers often prefer the security of full ownership and the absence of ground rent or service charges. It also tends to increase the property's value and appeal.

- Freehold flats: Be aware that whilst freehold is generally considered desirable, freehold flats are less so because many mortgage lenders won't lend against them.

59. WHAT INSURANCE DO I NEED?

Naturally this is important; when you buy a house there are several types of insurance to consider to protect both the property and your significant financial investment.

Buildings insurance

- What it covers: Buildings insurance covers the structure of your home, including the walls, roof, windows, and any permanent fixtures like kitchens or bathrooms. It also covers rebuilding costs if the property is damaged by fire, flooding, subsidence, or storms.

- When you need it: Buildings insurance is typically required by mortgage lenders as a condition of the loan, and you'll need to have it in place by the time you exchange contracts.

- Cost factors: The cost of buildings insurance depends on factors like the age and size of your home, its location, and the likelihood of risks such as flooding or subsidence (see Tip 28).

Contents insurance

- What it covers: This insurance protects your personal belongings, including furniture, electronics, clothing, and valuables, against risks such as theft, fire, or water damage. Contents insurance can be extended to cover accidental damage and items taken outside the home.

- When you need it: While not required by mortgage lenders, it is highly recommended, especially for protecting valuable personal belongings.

- What to consider: Make sure the policy provides enough coverage for the full value of your possessions, and check whether items like jewellery or electronics are covered outside the home.

Life insurance (with mortgage protection)

- What it covers: Life insurance with mortgage protection is designed to pay off your mortgage if you pass away during the term of the policy. The payout helps ensure your family doesn't lose the home due to unpaid mortgage debt.

- When you need it: Although not legally required, many homeowners take out this insurance for peace of mind, especially if they have dependents who would struggle to cover mortgage payments.

- Two main types: Level term - pays a fixed amount if you die within the policy term. Decreasing term - the payout decreases over time, matching the reducing balance of a repayment mortgage.

Income protection insurance

- What it covers: Income protection insurance provides you with a percentage of your income if you are unable to work due to illness, injury, or disability. This can help cover mortgage payments and other essential costs.

- When you need it: While not essential for everyone, it is worth considering, particularly if you are self-employed or do not have access to sick pay through your employer.

Critical illness cover

- What it covers: This type of insurance provides a lump sum payment if you are diagnosed with a serious illness, such as cancer or heart disease. The money can be used to cover mortgage payments, medical costs, or living expenses during recovery.

- When you need it: It's an optional policy but is often combined with life insurance for added protection. It can be especially important if your family relies on your income.

Mortgage payment protection insurance (MPPI)

- What it covers: MPPI is designed to cover your mortgage payments if you lose your job, are made redundant, or become unable to work due to illness or injury. Payments are usually made for a fixed period (typically 12-24 months).

- When you need it: It's not a legal requirement, but it can be a useful safety net, especially for those who want peace of mind about mortgage payments if they lose their income.

Legal expenses insurance

- What it covers: This insurance covers legal fees related to property disputes, such as boundary disagreements, planning permission conflicts, or problems with tenants (for buy-to-let properties). It is often an add-on to home insurance policies.

- When you need it: Consider it if you want to protect yourself against potentially expensive legal fees related to property issues.

Indemnity insurance

- What it covers: It protects homebuyers from legal or financial risks related to property defects, such as missing building regulations approval, lack of planning permission, rights of way issues, or restrictive covenant breaches. It covers costs arising from enforcement action but does not fix defects or cover future issues.

- When you need it: It is typically used when a property has a legal issue that could be costly or time-consuming to resolve but has a low likelihood of enforcement. Mortgage lenders often accept indemnity insurance as an alternative to obtaining retrospective approvals.

- Point to note: The issue must not have been alerted to the potential claimant/enforcer e.g. the local authority, as this would void the policy.

60. WHAT IS AN ARCHITECT'S CERTIFICATE (PCC)?

An Architect's Certificate or a "Professional Consultant's Certificate (PCC)" is a document issued by a qualified architect or building professional to confirm that a new-build or renovation project has been constructed to a good standard in accordance with the specification, plans and statutory consents. This certificate is typically used particularly for smaller developments or self-build projects, to assure buyers and lenders of the structural integrity and quality of the building. It is worth checking with your lender if they require a certificate or a specific guarantee such as an NHBC warranty which is different, (see Tip 12).

For the buyer, the PCC is usually legally transferrable to them and can help protect them if construction defects or issues arise after the purchase, but this shouldn't be confused with a building warranty. It is advisable to ask for a copy of the PCC issuer's professional indemnity insurance and check the level of cover.

Validity period

PCCs are typically valid for six years from the date of completion. If any structural defects occur within this period due to poor design or construction, the architect (or professional who issued the certificate) could be found negligent.

Alternative to a structural warranty

It is often used as a more cost-effective alternative to traditional new-build warranties, such as those provided by the NHBC. While a PCC does not offer financial coverage like a warranty, it is generally accepted by many lenders and serves as proof that the property has been built to proper standards.

Limitation of liability

A PCC generally does not provide insurance for latent defects or future problems, as a structural warranty might. It simply certifies that the architect has inspected the building at key stages and deems it compliant. Buyers should be aware of this difference.

61. WHAT IF IT'S A LISTED BUILDING?

If you're buying a listed building the chances are your new home will be full of character and charm, but there are important considerations, legal obligations, and potential challenges you need to address. A listed building is one that is legally protected due to its historical or architectural significance, and this affects what you can and cannot do with the property.

Understand the listing grade

The grade of the listing affects the level of control the local authority has over changes you can make to the building.

- Grade I: Buildings of exceptional interest. Only around 2.5% of listed buildings are Grade I and these are often commercial/public buildings or stately homes.

- Grade II*: Particularly important buildings of more than special interest (around 5.5% of listed buildings).

- Grade II: Buildings of national importance and special interest (most common, around 92% of listed buildings).

Obtaining listed building consent for alterations

- Any alterations, repairs, or extensions to a listed building usually require Listed Building Consent from the local planning authority/conservation officer, including for internal changes.

- Unauthorised changes could lead to enforcement action, fines, or even the requirement to reverse the work. To emphasise this point, if you buy a listed building that has had unauthorised work carried out to it at any time in the past, you could be forced to rectify it, i.e. you inherit the problem.

- Always consult the local conservation officer before planning any alterations.

Research maintenance responsibilities

- Listed buildings often require specialist materials and craftsmanship to maintain their historical character, which can be more expensive than regular maintenance.

- Investigate whether the building has any previous planning or consent issues, as this could impact your future obligations.

Understand restrictions on modern additions

- Adding modern conveniences such as double glazing, solar panels, or extensions may be limited or require creative solutions to ensure they don't detract from the building's historical character.

- In some cases, exceptions can be made for listed buildings which don't meet the standards required by more modern buildings, for example in respect of energy efficiency, but this is on a case-by-case basis.

Insurance costs and limitations

- Listed building insurance can be more expensive due to the potential higher costs of repairs and the need for specialist materials and skills. Find out who the current owner insures with to get an estimate of cost.

Financial grants and support

- You may be eligible for grants or financial assistance to help with the upkeep and maintenance of a listed building. However, these grants are often limited and competitive and may come with onerous clauses such as the requirement to grant occasional public access.

- Contact organisations like Historic England, CADW (Wales), or your local authority to inquire about available support.

Risks and challenges

- Legal liabilities: To reiterate as the new owner, you inherit any existing breaches of listed building regulations, so ensure your solicitor checks for any past unauthorised works.

- Resale potential: Listed buildings can be harder to sell due to the restrictions on modifications and the potential for higher maintenance costs. On the other hand, if the right buyer falls in love with the character of your building, the preservation of it can be a selling point.

- Future work costs: Again, to point out repairs and renovations often require special materials and skilled labour, making maintenance more expensive than for non-listed properties.

Steps to take

- Get a survey (see Tip 3): Instruct a building surveyor with experience in listed buildings to identify issues and potential costs.

- Speak with the local authority conservation officer about the property's status and any future plans you have for renovation or restoration.

- Ensure all previous work on the property was properly authorised with listed building consent.

62. WHAT IF IT IS IN AN AONB OR CONSERVATION AREA?

If the house you're buying is located in an Area of Outstanding Natural Beauty (AONB) or a Conservation Area, there are additional legal protections and planning restrictions designed to preserve the area's special architectural or natural characteristics. These designations can affect what you can do with the property and how you maintain or alter it.

Area of Outstanding Natural Beauty (AONB)

An AONB is a designated area with significant landscape value that is protected for conservation purposes. Restrictions are not usually as strict as those which apply to properties in designated National Parks.

Restrictions

- Development and alterations are more strictly controlled in an AONB than those outside of one. Any significant changes to the property, especially external alterations or extensions, are likely to require planning permission. This is because the area's scenic beauty must be preserved, and any development should not harm the landscape's character.

- You may be expected to pay particular attention to using materials and designs that are sympathetic to the natural environment, such as using local stone or specific building techniques.

- If the property includes land, there may be further restrictions on how it can be used, especially if it's considered important to the landscape.

What you should do

- Consult the Local Planning Authority (LPA): Always check with the local authority before making any changes to the property to ensure compliance with AONB regulations.

- Consider environmental impact: Even minor changes may require planning permission if they could have an impact on the landscape, such as installing solar panels or new fencing.

Conservation Area

A Conservation Area is a designated zone of architectural or historic interest where the local council aims to preserve the character and appearance of the area. Conservation Areas often include older, historically significant buildings or areas with unique architectural features.

Restrictions

In Conservation Areas, you often need planning permission for any significant external changes, even if they wouldn't normally require permission in non-conservation areas. This can include:

- Replacing windows or doors.
- Adding or altering rooflines (e.g., adding dormer windows).
- Extensions, even small ones.
- Changing external materials or colours.
- Demolition: Even partial demolition, such as removing part of a wall, may require consent.
- Trees in conservation areas are often protected, and you may need permission to prune or remove them.

What you should do

- Check with the Local Authority: Before carrying out any works, check with the local planning authority. They will provide guidance on what changes are permitted.

- Understand the Conservation Area Appraisal: Many local authorities publish a Conservation Area Appraisal, which outlines the special character of the area and what features are considered important. Familiarise yourself with this document to understand the restrictions on your property.

Additional considerations

- Properties in AONBs or Conservation Areas may command higher prices due to their scenic or historic value. However, the planning restrictions can limit what you can do with the property and may equally put some buyers off.

- Be prepared to use specific materials or techniques in any repair or extension work, which may be more expensive.

- You'll likely need to take extra care to maintain the property's character and heritage, which can sometimes result in higher maintenance costs.

63. WHY IS IT IMPORTANT TO CONSIDER THE SURROUNDING LAND USE?

Considering the surrounding land use when buying a house is sensible as it can directly impact your quality of life, property value, and potential future developments.

Impact on property value

The surrounding land use can significantly affect the future value of your property. For example, if the adjacent land is not designated for further development, it could maintain or increase the value of your home. However, if the land is zoned for industrial or commercial development, future developments like factories or shopping centres could lower property values due to noise, pollution, or increased traffic.

Neighbouring developments

Understanding how the land around your property is used or zoned is crucial because future developments could dramatically change the character of the area. For example, if there are plans for large housing estates or commercial developments, you may experience increased noise, congestion, and pressure on local services. Conversely, nearby green spaces or conservation areas might enhance your enjoyment of the property and support long-term value.

Environmental factors

Flood risk, subsidence, or soil contamination from surrounding land uses can pose a direct threat to your property. Land that was previously used for industrial purposes may carry environmental risks that could impact your property's safety and value. Checking local environmental assessments or historical land use records can highlight such issues.

Quality of life

The type of land use in surrounding areas affects your day-to-day living. Proximity to green spaces, parks, or recreational facilities can enhance your living experience. However, being near commercial zones, industrial estates, or high-traffic areas can negatively impact your quality of life by increasing noise, pollution, or traffic congestion.

CLOSE

Congratulations. If you have drudged through this book right to the end you have demonstrated that you are seriously committed to buying a house. Whilst there are far more exciting things you could have done with your time (such as research what colour towels you will buy for your new bathroom), you have empowered yourself with a lot of the important information you will need on your home buying journey and have armed yourself ready to ask the right questions.

In all seriousness, if this book can help you feel more confident to navigate the process, then that would be a win. I would feel very proud if I stumbled across your copy of this book and it was covered with notes, highlights and folded pages. This might demonstrate that you haven't just read the information; you have applied it.

I genuinely hope that you not only find, but buy, the best home for you right now, and it supports you in all the ways that you hope in the next exciting chapter of your life.

Wishing you the very best.

Anna

SPREAD THE WORD

If you found this book helpful, please consider leaving a review online and recommending it to family and friends - it could make a real difference in their home buying journey. Thank you.

GLOSSARY

Abstract of Title

A summary of the legal documents that prove ownership of a property.

Agreed Notice

An entry on the Land Registry Title Register made with the property owner's consent or proven evidence, protecting a third party's interest in the property.

Agreement in Principle (AIP)

A document from a mortgage lender confirming how much they may lend you based on your financial circumstances.

Architect's Certificate

Also known as s Professional Consultant's Certificate, (PCC), is a document issued by a qualified architect, surveyor, or engineer confirming that a new build or conversion complies with building regulations and approved plans. Often required by mortgage lenders, it serves as an alternative to a structural warranty, offering assurance of the property's structural integrity. Typically valid for six years.

Auction Property

A property sold through an auction process, often with a requirement to exchange contracts immediately after the auction ends.

Bridging Loan

A short-term loan used to "bridge" the gap between the purchase of a new property and the sale of an existing one.

Building Regulations

Standards for design and construction to ensure safety and compliance with national policies.

Building Parts and Common Issues

- **Roof**: Includes tiles, slates, membranes, flashing, and gutters; common issues are leaks and missing tiles.
- **Walls**: Can be brick, stone, block, concrete, or timber; issues may include water ingress/damp symptoms and structural movement/cracks.
- **Windows**: Commonly double-glazed; issues can include condensation, rot, or broken seals.
- **Foundation**: The base of the building - usually in the ground; problems may include subsidence or settlement.
- **Plumbing**: Includes pipes, fixtures, and drainage; issues can involve leaks, blockages, or outdated systems.
- **Electrical System**: Wiring, sockets, and fuse boxes; potential issues include outdated wiring and overloaded circuits.
- **Floors**: Includes wood, concrete, steel structures; problems may include uneven surfaces, settlement, or rot.
- **Ceilings**: Can show signs of leaks or cracks, indicating structural or plumbing issues.

Buildings Insurance

Insurance that covers the cost of repairing damage to the structure of your property. A requirement for most mortgage lenders.

Buy-to-Let

A property purchased with the intention of renting it out to tenants.

Chain

A series of linked property sales where each transaction depends on the preceding one being completed.

Chain-Free
A property being sold without the seller needing to buy another property simultaneously, simplifying the transaction.

Charges Register
A section of a property's Land Registry title document that records any financial charges, such as mortgages, and other legal interests or restrictions affecting the property, including easements, restrictive covenants, or rights benefiting third parties.

Chattels
Tangible, movable personal property that is not fixed to land or buildings, such as furniture, vehicles, and equipment.

Commonhold
A form of property ownership in England and Wales where multi-unit buildings (e.g., flats) are owned as freehold units, with a Commonhold Association managing shared areas. It removes the need for leaseholds and avoids ground rent or lease expiry issues.

Completion
The final stage in the property-buying process when ownership is legally transferred to the buyer.

Completion Statement
A document provided by the solicitor detailing the financial breakdown of the property purchase, including all fees and costs.

Conveyancing
The legal process of transferring property ownership from the seller to the buyer.

Covenants

Legal agreements or restrictions tied to the property, often concerning land use or modifications.

Curtilage

The land directly surrounding a property, including areas like gardens or driveways, closely tied to its use and legally considered part of it.

Deposit

The amount of money paid upfront towards the purchase price of a property, typically 5-20% of the total cost.

Disbursements

Additional costs incurred during conveyancing, such as local authority searches or Land Registry fees.

Easement

A legal right allowing one property owner to use another's land for a specific purpose, such as access, drainage, or services. Easements are typically permanent and bind future owners of both the benefitting and burdened properties.

Energy Performance Certificate (EPC)

A document that rates the energy efficiency of a property and provides recommendations for improvement.

Equitable Charge

A financial interest in a property that secures the repayment of a debt or obligation, without transferring ownership or creating a legal mortgage.

Equity

The difference between the property's market value and the outstanding mortgage balance.

Exchange Deposit
A portion of the deposit paid at the time of exchanging contracts, typically 10% of the purchase price.

Exchange of Contracts
The point at which the buyer and seller become legally bound to complete the transaction.

First-Time Buyer
A person purchasing their first home who has not previously owned property.

Flying Freehold
A part of a freehold property that extends over or under another freehold, such as an overhanging room or structure. The property is not "mid-air" as the name implies, rather it overlaps. It may affect access, maintenance, and mortgage eligibility.

Freehold
Ownership of both the property and the land it stands on, without time limitations.

Gazumping
When a seller accepts a higher offer from another buyer after previously agreeing to a sale.

Gazundering
When a buyer reduces their offer just before contracts are exchanged.

Green Belt Land
Areas of open land around cities where development is restricted to preserve the natural environment.

Ground Rent

An annual fee paid by leaseholders to the freeholder as part of the lease agreement.

Indemnity Insurance

In relation to property it is a policy that protects owners from unforeseen risk and financial loss e.g. due to missing building regulations, restrictive covenants, or rights of way issues.

Landlord

A person or entity that owns a property and rents it out to a tenant in exchange for rent.

Land Registry

The government department responsible for recording property ownership in England and Wales.

Latent Defect

A hidden structural fault that isn't visible at purchase but may cause issues later, often due to poor workmanship or materials. Often covered by structural warranties or latent defects insurance.

Leasehold

Ownership of a property for a fixed term, but not the land it stands on. Leaseholders usually pay ground rent and service charges.

Legal Charge

A legally binding security interest registered against a property to secure the repayment of a loan, typically a mortgage. It gives the lender the right to take possession or sell the property if the borrower fails to meet their repayment obligations.

Lender's Valuation

An assessment carried out by the mortgage lender to ensure the property's value aligns with the loan amount requested.

Loan-to-value Ratio (LTV)

The percentage of a loan compared to the property value. Calculated as:

LTV = (Loan Amount ÷ Property Value) × 100.

Example: (Mortgage £150,000 ÷ Property Value £200,000) × 100 = 75%.

A higher LTV means more borrowing relative to value, increasing the lender's risk.

Money Laundering

The process of hiding money obtained through unlawful activities by processing it through the financial system, such as buying and selling a house, thus obscuring its origin.

Mortgage Agreement

The formal contract between a borrower and a lender outlining the terms of a loan for purchasing property.

Mortgage Broker

A professional who helps buyers find and apply for a suitable mortgage.

NHBC Certificate

A warranty provided by the National House Building Council for new homes, (see "Structural Warranty"), typically covering structural defects for ten years. Other warranty providers are also available.

Offer

The price a buyer proposes to pay for a property.

Overage

A clause in a property sale contract that entitles the seller to receive additional payment in the future if the property's value increases due to certain events, such as planning permission being granted.

Party Wall
A wall shared between two properties, often subject to specific agreements for maintenance or modifications.

Planning Permission
Consent granted by a local authority for changes to or development of a property or land.

Probate Sale
The sale of a property owned by someone who has passed away, often managed by an executor of the estate.

Professional Consultant's Certificate, (PCC)
Also known as an Architect's Certificate, is a document issued by a qualified architect, surveyor, or engineer confirming that a new build or conversion complies with building regulations and approved plans. Often required by mortgage lenders, it serves as an alternative to a structural warranty, offering assurance of the property's structural integrity. Typically valid for six years.

Positive Covenant
A legal obligation attached to the property owner to perform specific actions, such as maintaining a boundary, contributing to shared costs, or carrying out repairs. Unlike restrictive covenants, they do not automatically bind future owners unless explicitly agreed.

Redemption Fee
A charge applied by some lenders for repaying a mortgage early.

Restrictive Covenant

A negative legal condition attached to a property that limits how it can be used, for example restricting extensions, businesses, or alterations.

They typically "run with the land," meaning they remain attached to the property when it is transferred to another owner.

Right to Manage (RTM)

A legal right in England and Wales allowing leaseholders of a residential building to take over the management of their property from the landlord, without needing to prove fault, by forming a Right to Manage company under the Commonhold and Leasehold Reform Act 2002.

Searches

Investigations carried out by conveyancers to check for any issues affecting the property, such as local planning proposals or environmental risks.

Shared Ownership Scheme

A government-backed scheme allowing buyers to purchase a percentage of a property and pay rent on the remainder.

Sitting Tenant

Is a tenant already renting a premises when the landlord sells it. They remain in the property after ownership changes or a tenancy ends, often with legal protection particularly against eviction or rent increases. Sometimes referred to as a "tenant in situ".

Snagging List

A list of defects or unfinished work in a newly built property, typically provided by the buyer to the developer for rectification.

Stamp Duty Land Tax (SDLT)

A tax paid on property purchases over a certain value in England and Northern Ireland.

Structural Engineer's Report

A detailed analysis conducted by a Structural Engineer or possibly a Chartered Building Surveyor to assess suspected structural issues in the property. Can be requested by mortgage lenders following valuation/survey.

Structural Warranty

An insurance policy that covers defects in the structural integrity of a new build or converted property for a set period, typically 10 years. It is required by most mortgage lenders. Also see "Professional Consultant's Certificate".

Subject to Contract

Indicates that an agreement has been reached in principle but is not yet legally binding.

Survey

An inspection of a property's condition, often carried out by a Chartered Surveyor.

Types of Surveys

- **Condition Report**: A basic survey suitable for newer properties, highlighting urgent issues but without extensive detail.

- **Homebuyer Report / Home Survey**: A more detailed survey, including the property's condition, potential issues, and potentially including a market valuation.

- **Building Survey**: The most comprehensive survey, ideal for older or unusual properties, detailing structural and maintenance issues.

Tenant

A person or entity that rents a property from a landlord under a tenancy agreement.

Tenant In-situ

Any tenant remaining in a property during or after a sale meaning the new owner inherits the tenancy agreement. The term "Sitting tenant" is similar but would tend to mean tenants have stronger legal protections.

Title Deeds

A collection of legal documents that historically proved ownership and detailed the rights, obligations, and boundaries of a property. While they are less critical since the introduction of land registration, (Title Register/Plan), they may still hold valuable information particularly for unregistered land.

Title Register

An official document maintained by the Land Registry that provides details about a property, including ownership, property description, and any legal rights or restrictions (such as those in the Charges Register). It serves as proof of ownership and outlines the property's legal status.

Title Plan

An official map produced by the Land Registry that shows the general boundaries of a registered property.

Under Offer

A property status indicating that an offer has been made and accepted, but contracts have not yet been exchanged.

Unilateral Notice

An entry on the Land Registry Title Register that protects a third party's interest in a property without the property owner's consent.

Vacant Possession

The legal right to take possession of a property free from occupants, tenants, or any belongings that could prevent full use.

Variable-Rate Mortgage

A type of mortgage where the interest rate fluctuates based on changes in the lender's standard variable rate (SVR).

Vendor

The person or entity selling the property.

REFERENCES

2024 Leasehold Reform Bill

2024 Renters (Reform) Bill (applies to England only)

abi.org.uk

BRE Digest 245, Rising Damp in Walls

BRE Digest 251, Assessment of damage in low-rise buildings

BRE Pocket Handbook, Trevor Rushton, 2016

britishgas.co.uk

bt.com

Building Safety Act 2022

Buying and Selling Your Own Home, Frances James, 2024

cadw.gov.wales

Can rent; can't buy - The affordability of renting and buying for workers across Great Britain – Oct 2024, Zoopla/ONS

citizensadvice.org.uk

clc-uk.org

Commonhold and Leasehold Reform Act 2002

consumercode.co.uk

Cracking in Buildings, RB Bonshor & LL Bonshor, 1996

electricalsafetyfirst.org.uk

Energy Act 2011

Energy Performance of Buildings (England and Wales) Regulations 2012

england.shelter.org.uk

energysavingtrust.org.uk

fensa.org.uk

Fire Safety Act 2021

flood-warning-information.service.gov.uk

floodre.co.uk

gassaferegister.co.uk

gov.uk
gov.uk/government/organisations/environment-agency
gov.wales
historicengland.org.uk
hoa.org.uk
Housing Act 2004
Housing and Planning Act 2016
How to Buy a House Without Killing Anyone, Andrew Boast FMAAT, 2023
hse.gov.uk
labc.co.uk
landlord and Tenant Act 1985 (amended)
Land Registration Act 2002
landscapesforlife.org.uk
lawsociety.org.uk
Leasehold Reform, Housing and Urban Development Act 1993
lease-advice.org
local.gov.uk
moneyadviceservice.org.uk
moneyhelper.org.uk
moneysavingexpert.com
naturalresources.wales
ofcom.org.uk
ofgem.gov.uk
ofwat.gov.uk
ons.gov.uk
Party Wall etc. Act 1996
planningportal.co.uk
property-care.org
propertymark.co.uk
ramblers.org.uk

Home Buyer's Essentials

rics.org/uk

selfbuild.wales

smp.org.uk

sra.org.uk

tax.service.gov.uk

thameswater.co.uk

Town and Country Planning Act 1990

ukradon.org

Watts Pocket Handbook, Trevor Rushton, 2016

which.co.uk

Your Step by Step Guide to Moving House, Help for Movers by Lisa Rogerson

NOTES

Home Buyer's Essentials

....flicked to the back of the book and wondered why there are 63 tips, not 50 as advertised?....refer to page 6.

First Edition, England & Wales

2025, GREDU

All rights reserved

ISBN 978-1-0369-1143-0

Printed in Dunstable, United Kingdom

64782768R10127